To Sis

With dearest love,

Charles
Harry Jo
Charles Graves
Vicki
and
David

March 10, 1971

I REMAIN UNVANQUISHED

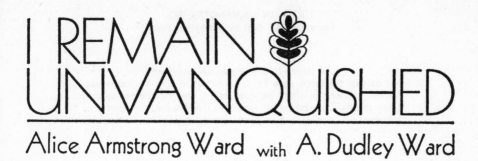

I REMAIN UNVANQUISHED

Alice Armstrong Ward with A. Dudley Ward

ABINGDON PRESS
nashville & new york

ISBN 0-687-18550-5

Library of Congress Catalog Card Number: 76-112887

SET UP, PRINTED, AND BOUND BY THE
PARTHENON PRESS, AT NASHVILLE,
TENNESSEE, UNITED STATES OF AMERICA

CONTENTS

PREFACE

Our purpose in writing this book is to share with a wide community of people, both laity and clergy, the evidence, at least to us, that God through the Holy Spirit does lead in ways not always recognized, often unusual and even beyond belief. While one of us, Alice, will tell the story, because in so many ways it is her story, the other, Dudley, has been an intimate participant in her experiences for more than half her life.

As Alice narrates, we will frankly share our experiences, those of two persons from similar yet diverse backgrounds, with substantially different psychological and spiritual approaches, certainly in the initial stages of our relationship, and with gifts different both in meaning and expression.

The book will illustrate the way in which life situations of family, pain, vocation, physical crisis, involvement with others, and death itself become part of the unfolding encounter with the living God.

It was also our intention to show some dimensions of the movement toward renewal within two individuals and within the church we love. While quite simple, in its presuppositions and expressions, the book comes out of a depth and breadth of experience constantly made rich with extensive study, reading, and discussion of the major literature on the Bible, theology, ethics, and church history.

We hope that this book will serve as a basis for discussion and understanding by many people in their own personal and group search for a sense of direction and awareness of the presence of God. Such a quest requires openness to appropriate the spiritual power available to all men.

We cannot possibly acknowledge all the people who have contributed to the development of our lives. Nothing that has happened has taken place in a vacuum. People of all sorts, conditions, and races—both in and out of the church—play an integral part in the entire drama. This adds wonder, and at points terror, to the experience of deeper and deeper involvement with God.

Our lives have been directed toward the realization that each day lived together and each day with God is entirely precious—because it could be the last. The ability to live within this margin has not come easily, nor has it come quickly, but —as the book will indicate—by a slow process in our lives, intimately involved with each other, but also autonomous and open to whatever guidance God gives through his Spirit.

We have come to the conclusion that the usual narrow margins imposed upon the disciplines of prayer and healing must be broadened and seen in their wider context of social dimensions. The thorough-going involvement in the drama of human events, especially as they have unfolded in the past twenty-five years, has confronted us with the fact that the crusader cannot act with confidence and compassion unless he is developing profound spiritual disciplines. This linking of the individual's inner spiritual resources and the involvement in social action has been one of the exciting discoveries of these decades.

We hope that this sharing of our experiences may help

others, especially young people, in their search. Some persons may believe they have approached the point of no return. But we have known the heartening reality that life can always be renewed and become something quite different from what a person had anticipated, or move in directions different from those he had set.

The title is taken from the Armstrong (Scotland) family coat of arms. Alice is a member of that clan.

The efforts which have gone into building two lives and into writing this book will be amply rewarded if some other persons find, through their reading and further searching, this life of spiritual adventure.

Alice and Dudley Ward

1 DISAPPOINTMENT AND JOY

"Your baby is dead."

The crisp statement from a young doctor who had attended me for more than seven months during my pregnancy for our third child chilled me as much as the cold, icy winter's night outside the office on this Valentine's Day in 1951.

For a number of weeks I suspected that something was wrong, but the doctor had insisted that the baby was developing normally, that he could detect signs of the life within my body. The news he gave me and my husband, Dudley, who had accompanied me to the doctor's office, seemed to shock him as much as it did us. Alarmed because he believed the baby might have been dead for several days, or even more than a week, the young doctor advised us to go immediately to a specialist, in spite of the late hour and the sleety, icy night.

Together Dudley and I immediately visited a specialist only a short distance from the doctor's office. He confirmed the diagnosis and in a cold, calculating way, it seemed to me, advised my entrance the next morning to a hospital for surgical removal of the fetus.

How we agonized during the long, treacherous drive back

13

to our Roosevelt, Long Island, home where we had to give the horrible news to my mother, who had remained with our two daughters, Dianne, almost seven, and Beverly, four. A wonderfully gracious, deeply spiritual person, Mother had come to stay with us and care for me during the final weeks of the pregnancy. With eleven children of her own, all born at home, and now with twenty-five grandchildren, she was well prepared. Each child, no matter how many she had seen or assisted, became a great wonder and joy to this woman, who had an overflowing capacity for motherhood.

Dudley and I shared the stunning news with Mother; during that long night we pondered our next steps. Sometime that night we decided we could not accept the young doctor's and the specialist's diagnoses as the whole truth. This became the first of many times throughout our lives when we confronted the need to bring our own critical judgment and insight to bear—even upon professional advice.

Gradually we felt with assurance that we should not return to either of the doctors who had examined me that evening or go to the hospital they recommended. Instead we decided to travel to Brooklyn, New York, for examination and treatment at the Methodist Hospital, which for years had symbolized the church in its finest expression of the healing ministry.

Acting on our decision, Dudley took me to the church-related hospital. There we met a great man, Dr. Stanley Hall, then a chief in obstetrics and gynecology. He immediately evidenced interest in my case. His concern and obvious skill gave to both Dudley and me new confidence that, even though we faced a grave situation, we could confront it with hope.

My admission to the Methodist Hospital became part of the unfolding story of my own and Dudley's spiritual awareness. For almost three weeks a large medical team performed extensive testing in an attempt to determine conclusively the truth of my condition. As the tests progressed, they became increasingly certain that the other two physicians had erred in their diagnoses.

During my stay in the hospital my minister-husband experienced some of his deepest relationships with fellow clergymen. Later he told me that this experience made him realize that his technical preparation for the ministry was not adequate to serve people facing a crisis such as ours. In the years which followed, this became part of the search—to find ways in which pastors can really help persons in periods of similar crisis.

At the hospital I was in a general ward with four other mothers who had just given birth. Happily enjoying the thrill of new life and motherhood, they believed that I showed all the appearances of pregnancy and would soon share their joy. I had difficulty, and so did they, accepting the fact that something was seriously wrong.

This, then, became one of the first occasions on which I had to adopt a positive relationship to life's unpredictable possibilities. I had to call on resources by which to live in the presence of the ecstatic joy of the new mothers and the hard reality of my own condition. Originally I, too, had anticipated joy. Eventually the doctors suggested a move to a private room to alleviate such tensions.

After further tests the doctors concluded that I had not been pregnant and that, far from a dead child, the swelling was an extensive tumor, which at this point seemed to them to be the dreaded ovarian mold. This diagnosis added a completely new complexion to our crisis and demanded another readjustment of our thinking about the strange events in the unreal world of medicine and physical disease. When the crisis became more acute, and the doctors obviously had some doubt as to whether or not they could save my life, my husband and I had to confront another first in our life experience—the possibility of death.

Dr. Hall shared our crisis with great understanding and feeling. Now we began to understand the interdependence of spiritual power and the healing which comes through reputable physicians and medical procedures. We also realized that a patient in crisis can easily become a test case for some doctors and attendants and be depersonalized through the extensive daily examinations. Without the compassion and capacity of Dr. Hall, I could easily have lost both respect for and hope in doctors and their methods.

After debating whether to risk surgery, Dr. Hall and his associates decided on a last resort as the abdominal pressure from the growth became more intense. About six o'clock one evening I was "packed"—a procedure the doctors hoped would stimulate a self-expulsion of the mold—with the understanding that I would have no medication, not even an aspirin, for twelve hours. Another ice storm had created such hazardous conditions that Dudley could not get into the city, so I suffered through the hours with no company and intense pain.

As midnight approached, a shadow appeared in the doorway of my room and quietly moved to the side of my bed. The visitor took my hand in his and held it for a time.

"Alice, I had to come."

As quickly as he had come, the man left the room. Amazingly, from that moment, the pain began to subside and I felt a calm peace within and without my body. At dawn, Dr. Hall entered the room to announce that he knew what he had to do. I would undergo immediate surgery.

That same morning, after Dudley had arrived, we learned that the shadowy figure who had come to my room at midnight was Pastor Jack Zeiter of Hanson Place Methodist Church in Brooklyn. He had been in bed at home, awakened, and told his wife that he had to visit the hospital. "It's Alice Ward," he had told his wife. "I must go to her." The storm kept him from getting his car into the street and taxis had become unavailable

16

to the hospital some seven blocks away. There he visited me on the slippery roads, so the pastor walked from his apartment and consulted with Dr. Hall. Their prayers gave the doctor spiritual direction.

After the operation Dr. Hall visited with Dudley and me, and, when I could understand, gave us a detailed explanation of the surgery. He told us they had found a number of growths in the reproductive organs including a massive one in the uterus. They also had discovered the five-months fetus of a boy, which, in spite of the growths, was normal and healthy, but which had to be removed in the operation.

Colleagues advised a complete hysterectomy, but Dr. Hall strongly resisted this, feeling the influence of factors not explainable simply on surgical grounds. He decided to take the responsibility of a resectioning of the uterus and a replacing of the organs after removing, to the best of his ability, the tumors.

Surprisingly, I recovered quickly after the operation. During the recovery period I learned that my mother had not removed any of the equipment or stopped the preparations for the new child we had anticipated. She insisted, in fact, that I complete all the sewing which I had begun for the new baby and put away the clothing for future use.

As recovery became more evident and the situation in the home returned to normal, and consultations with Dr. Hall were going on, it was apparent that the possibility of having another child should be faced. This was not without considerable questioning and some distress, for it was Dudley's general attitude that he did not wish me to go through a similar event and subject the family and me to the kind of hazards through which I had been.

The matter came to a climax about two years later, following a trip to Europe in which we had new experiences and participated in events which were unfamiliar and delightful to us.

It was when I was kneeling beside the bed in prayer one

evening that I heard a voice saying to me, "You are healed, you are healed, you are healed," and the awareness seemed to be verified deep within my inner self. As I lay in bed that night, the realization kept sweeping over me that I was healed and that this healing encompassed my entire body. If this were true, I had no right to cling to the fear of pregnancy. I could have another child. For the next two nights, when I knelt in prayer, the same voice and the exact words were heard, "You are healed," three times in succession. A few days later, since this awareness was repeated, I could no longer confine it. I spoke about it to Dudley. He expressed the concern that he had had since the other disappointment. He did not want to involve me in anything that would have an element of further tragedy or heartache, but he did agree that I could go to see Dr. Hall and tell him about this prayer experience. The doctor went over the case very carefully and reviewed it for me. He told me many of the dangers that could be involved in such a venture, but recognized the chance that everything could work out, that it was possible that I was completely healed, that there could be a normal pregnancy and another child. A few months later I returned to Dr. Hall, and he confirmed the fact that I was pregnant and assured me of his very best medical care and concern during the months ahead.

On the morning of August 6, 1952, I experienced the joy I had missed during that last ill-fated pregnancy, as I watched the doctors perform a Caesarian section to lift our son, John, from my body. Later that day Dr. Hall visited my bedside and shared with me his wonderment at the miracle of healing.

"If I had not been the doctor who performed the extensive surgery over a year ago," he told me, "I could not have believed that a human hand had touched those organs of your body. They healed perfectly."

2 | A THREAD OF DIVINE GUIDANCE

With my healing and the birth of our son, John, life took on new meaning as my husband and I contemplated the events of our years together. We began to understand that a close relationship exists between disappointment and fulfillment, sorrow and joy, life and death, hazard and security, fear and faith. Through our first vivid encounter with these ultimate realities of life, we glimpsed a thread of divine guidance which extended through all our experiences.

That thread reached back into Canada, where we both were born and reared. While distinctive in their origins, our families had certain things in common—the religious interests of our parents, commitment to the church as a religious home in which the family could develop, rigorous attention to the standards of morality characteristic of a conservative theological position, and a great desire to make a contribution to society.

My own family with eleven children, seven of them boys, faced a crisis when my father died at the age of forty-nine. His death placed a great burden on the older children and taxed the spiritual and physical vitality of my mother as she readjusted her life. Dudley's family, while not facing such a climactic event, struggled for economic security during the depression. Economic stress profoundly affected our lives as members of both families worked to eke out a living in those difficult days. A great desire for intellectual development through formal education grew from these early years.

I believe the thread of divine guidance also encompassed our courtship and marriage. I met Dudley while attending a meeting at a publishing house in downtown Toronto. As a friend and I struggled with a manual elevator, a young man wearing an English bowler suddenly appeared and said he would take over the controls. As he stepped into the elevator, I felt a strange inner knowledge that this man would somehow become involved in my life. Frankly, I was not overly thrilled with the thought because he did not, at this first encounter, much appeal to me. Later I was formally introduced to him at a church meeting and learned that he was working for his Chartered Accountant's degree, an apprenticeship which included work at the office and weekly study papers completed at home. I offered to help him type the reports and he accepted, so I soon found myself working night hours and weekends to research, as well as type, the papers, and mail them back across the city to his home.

The courtship moved slowly. Dudley's income in the accountant's office prohibited week-night dates, and even on weekends we frequently just took long walks, bought a hamburger and divided it. We did go to church together at other times, but our relationship remained essentially one of work. In spite of that, perhaps unknown to us, a profound degree of love had begun to develop between us. After some time Dudley received his degree and moved to the United States to pursue his business career, which involved work in New York's financial district, a variety of industrial pursuits, and development of land on Maryland's Eastern Shore. I broke off my relationship with him at this time, as I advanced my own business career and wanted a time of separation to discover the depth of our involvement.

During this period I began to realize that a mutual devotion to the Christian faith added a dimension to our relationship. I was much more certain in my faith than Dudley, who had entered a period of deep questioning, almost cynicism, about religion, especially the narrow confines of the conservative positions he had known. These two streams of religious life, however, did not harm but rather complemented our relationship. Dudley's analytical approach, his questions and deep doubts that disturbed him, did not detract from my own convictions. Instead, his searchings broadened and enlarged my own faith, giving it a scope which my earlier religious experiences had not offered.

Apparently Dudley weighed our differences and decided that I should become a part of his life, perhaps adding certain understandings and experiences he did not have. One evening he came to the clubhouse where I lived, and when I came into the reception room, handed me a nicely wrapped gift with the simple, direct, and almost unromantic statement, "I love you, Alice." Later we talked about wedding plans and both admitted reservations about life together. I personally wondered how I would fit into the new life that Dudley had begun to build for himself in the United States; I wondered, too, about differences in religious and social attitudes. While we shared our questions, however, we both sensed the presence of an inescapable force which had brought us together. Both of us had reached our late twenties, so this decision for a dramatic change in our lives had not come easily.

After the wedding in September, 1942, we immediately settled in our new home on the eastern shore of Maryland. The first big hurdle of our marriage came in a vocational struggle. Dudley had begun to evaluate his business relationships; the man with whom my husband worked had unique business imagination but expressed skepticism about many of the standards we felt were important. Dudley and I had also become acquainted with The Methodist Church and some of its leaders, who made quite an impression on him. Furthermore, my searching husband read the Social Creed of The Methodist Church one day. It captivated his imagination with its involvement of religion in society and forced him to re-evaluate his position on the church he could join.

That divine guidance was again at work, moving us toward a vocational change that would dramatically alter our lives as Dudley left a high executive position, with ample salary and a good future, to return to school for the long, hard pursuit of education—and to serve a local church along with his studies.

Following this decision, which received support from officials and members of the Peninsula Annual Conference, Dudley was assigned a student appointment in the rolling hills of northern Delaware. Ebenezer Church, five miles from Newark, stood in the beautiful countryside, a white frame building housing a congregation of 125, whose love and simple tastes added a warmth and stimulation to life. While serving the congregation, Dudley went to the University of Delaware for a Bachelor's Degree in philosophy and psychology, then continued his work for a Master's Degree in sociology and economics, preparing for a dimly envisioned unique church ministry.

On the Saturday night before Labor Day, 1944, only weeks after we had moved to Ebenezer Church, the parsonage telephone rang.

"Hello, Dudley. It's Ernie. I'm going through Washington on my way to Europe and have the weekend free. Thought I'd look you up."

We were thrilled to hear the familiar voice of Ernest Sullivan, Dudley's best friend from boyhood, and quickly arranged for the new infantry officer to visit us. A professional musician,

Ernie agreed to sing a solo at the worship service the next day.

In the morning our congregation filled the church. I stood at the entrance with Dianne, our seven-months old baby, in my arms. As Ernie stood to sing "Spirit of God," a vivid memory flashed into my mind. I recalled an evening two years before when I had stood in the doorway of the club where I lived to say good-bye to Ernie as he went to Texas to join his army unit.

"I don't know when I will see you again," he said as he turned to go.

My answer came without any conscious thoughts.

"Oh, I do know when you'll see me again. It will be two years from now. Dudley and I will have taken our first church and he'll be preaching his first sermon of that church year. We'll have a baby and you'll visit the church and even sing a solo."

Ernie looked at me as though I were a bit crazy, and I was as amazed as he at this strange prediction.

"Dudley Ward is going to make it in the business world," Ernie reminded me, "not in the ministry."

Later that Sunday morning at Ebenezer Church, when Ernie and I stood alone, he asked, "Did you ever tell Dudley what you told me two years ago?"

"No, I never did. I never told anyone but you that I knew this day could come."

"Don't you want to tell him about it now that it's happened?"

"No, I really don't want him to know because I want this decision he has made to be his. I don't want him to think he took this step because of some prediction I made or some premonition I had. I believe I received this knowledge so that in the time of decision I would be prepared for it and ready to make the adjustment. Knowing it was the will of God for our lives, I could adjust in a constructive way and enter the new life convinced that God had directed this decision and would continue his guidance in the years ahead."

However, that decision to serve the church and return to school for the necessary education didn't end the temptation to return to the business world or to use the new educational achievements for economic gain. Frankly, the economics of serving Ebenezer Church almost tripped us.

The salary reduction to $1,200 shocked us, and the parsonage, though pleasant in the warmth of summer, barely kept out the cold winter winds, had no decent furnace in the rat-infested basement. It *did* have all the inconveniences of an old, ramshackle frame country house. Dudley's educational costs and the weekly bills incurred in raising two little girls—our second daughter, Beverly, was born in 1946—became stark realities which we had not anticipated. Still, we determined that we should not borrow, for any purpose, from anyone.

To sustain our family, Dudley and I planted a garden, kept chickens, bought a freezer and filled it with low-cost large quantities of meat. We both spent weeks during the summer, in our spare time, preserving and freezing vegetables from the garden and fruits from the college farm. Obviously, we benefited from the exercise and the pioneer living experience.

While I had an inner awareness of Dudley's destiny in the church from the beginning of our relationship, I experienced difficulty in adjusting to our new way of life. I had also worked for ten years and enjoyed the pleasure of financial freedom. Now, as a minister's wife, I had to lead a life of discipline, both social and economic. However, I knew this was the right path, and thus accepted and adjusted to the hardship.

When new business opportunities came, as Dudley neared the close of his college work, I felt and shared the struggle of his decisions. I don't recall ever wavering from the clearness of our calling and the destiny of Christ for our lives. I did not remove myself from the struggle of his decisions; these were our decisions, for we realized that increased income would eliminate many of the pressures and limitations we experienced during these years.

I knew that I influenced Dudley a great deal, that many times my deep conviction held him to a certain way of thinking. Others also understood this, and several times they offered sizable gifts of money to me if I would urge him to return to business enterprises. I never did this. Though some of these offers came at times when we could have used more money, or at times when my health seemed about to fail, Dudley and I moved through these testings—and we gained new strength from them. Although it was difficult, we had a sense of victory as we resisted the temptations.

I believe that we met and overcame many of the crisis times —in health, finances, vocation—because we had begun to know the power of prayer. While we liked and wanted the "good things of life," the desire to possess them gradually faded and our paramount motive began to change our life.

How I admired my husband in these periods of decision making. Again and again he seemed to have marvelous opportunities offered him, and always he weighed carefully the opportunities and possibilities. Then he reached his decision in commitment to God's call, returning again to his church tasks with new enthusiasm and renewed zest. After making the decision, he never went back to question its rightness; that seemed obvious and filled him and his wife with new energy for the work to which we had committed our lives.

That work at Ebenezer Church offered a multitude of psychic and spiritual benefits to a young minister and his wife. These centered largely in the lives of certain persons.

Uncle Sammy Little, already eighty years old, active mentally and physically, of a conservative theological background but always open to new possibilities, took a genuine interest in the physical well-being of our family. He regularly came to the parsonage—almost by divine guidance, it often seemed, when we had emptied the larder or spent our last dollar—with a chicken, vegetables, or other food.

Uncle Sammy Little, however, gave us more than physical nourishment. The depth of his life became a channel for the guidance of God in our lives. Though physically aged and theologically conservative, Uncle Sammy had a keen and exciting mind and a wealth of experience, and challenged us to think about theology and our faith. He also had a tremendous respect for the office of pastor, and this helped my fledgling pastor-husband to see the responsibilities of the vocation he had decided to pursue.

John Buckingham, middle-aged when we met him, also made a priceless contribution to our lives. A rifle accident while John was in his mid-teens had made him a permanent invalid who could not attend to himself. His mind, however, remained alert, always comprehending new thoughts and ideas; he read much and developed a great capacity for spiritual power and sharing his knowledge.

At first Dudley thought he would minister to John. Soon he discovered that the invalid had much more to give, so they spent hours exchanging ideas, and John shared his reflections about people and human events as he watched them go by from his wheelchair and bed. For us John Buckingham became one of the first living illustrations of a truly whole person, and the concept of the whole person became central to the developing ministry I shared with my husband. Though limited in many ways, John had a freedom and initiative unknown to many people. He could really participate in life. Thus he helped us shape the ideas which became the foundations of our lives and ministry.

When Dudley completed the course work for a Master's Degree at the University of Delaware, we reached another turning point in our lives. Would he teach, return to business, or begin theological studies? Finally, we decided to go, in faith, to New York City, where Dudley would begin his theological education at Union Seminary. After Dudley sought and obtained a student pastorate in the New York East Conference, we left the rolling hills of Delaware on a hot summer day in 1947 to travel to the steaming, smelly, crowded downtown section of Brooklyn.

3 | THE THREAD WINDS THROUGH BROOKLYN AND BEYOND

I shall never forget the trip through the Holland Tunnel to midtown New York and then over to Brooklyn. Whatever glamor I had felt about the city soon dissolved as we faced numerous stark realities of our city life. The parsonage at Bethany Church, for instance, had only two rooms and one bedroom for our family of four, since two other families also rented some of its space. Its windows without screens allowed hordes of flies from the yards, alleys, and garbage to sweep into the stifling air of the apartment. So we began a rugged existence in the inner city.

Brooklyn changed the direction of my husband's ministry. During his pastorate there and his work at Union, Dudley received a superb education, had opportunities to re-evaluate his ministry, and encountered well-known persons in education, politics, and religion.

While Dudley plunged enthusiastically into his new life, I experienced a less engaging side. Our thirty-dollar-a-week salary didn't stretch very far, and the housing limitations plus a strange social environment made me feel as though we had taken our two little girls into a foreign land. I had a real mental and physical struggle to maintain the dignity and health of the family.

Dianne, three at this time, became a real source of courage for all of us. She and I, with Beverly in a stroller, often walked along the cluttered streets to a park where the children could sit in the grass, play, swing, and meet other children. The people who lived next to us in the row house were black and had three sons about the age of our girls. Since I had had little contact with black people, this was also a new relationship for me.

I remember so well the first time I walked to school with Dianne, wearing her best school clothes, her long blonde braids neatly tied with ribbons. As I left the house and opened the iron gate to the pavement, the mother of the black boy next door opened her gate. Because she had a small baby, she could not accompany her child to school. Hurriedly I pulled Dianne back into the house and stood there for a few seconds wondering what to do. Then I knew that I had to go out and give my other hand to the black boy. This began a new daily experience as, in the early days of Dianne's school life, I regularly walked with my blonde daughter holding one hand and our black neighbor boy holding the other.

In Brooklyn I learned about love in its universal depths in the hearts of mothers and children, regardless of color, station in life, or economic situation. I recognized that the love of this black mother for her three children equaled or perhaps exceeded my love for my own children.

Less than two weeks after we arrived in Brooklyn, violent cries from the street below our open barred window disturbed our rest one hot night. Dashing to see the cause of the commotion, we found two policemen unmercifully beating a Negro whom they had knocked to the ground. The man died there on the street. Incensed, Dudley called the precinct headquarters.

29

"You'd better keep your damn nose out of other people's business if you want to get along in this neighborhood," the desk sergeant growled.

Soon we found out that we lived and ministered in the midst of prostitution, narcotics, and the numbers racket. One Sunday afternoon two fine high school girls, not members of our church, came to ask Dudley's advice on what to do about dating boys in their school class who spent some of their afternoons in one of the nearby houses of prostitution. Another time a young boy came to him to ask about how he should handle the temptation to use drugs which he could get at school and on the street.

We also learned something about corrupt law enforcement. After a number of accidents in which six children were injured or killed, we inquired in the neighborhood about merchants using all the sidewalk and even part of the street to display their wares, a practice which forced the children into the streets.

"It's none of your business," the answer came again. Then we learned about the weekly payoffs, a completely unknown side of the law to us.

Following World War II a number of people came into our Brooklyn community from Eastern and Southern Europe. Many of them were Jewish and could not speak English. When the Jewish people established the Parkway Community Council, my activist husband became a member, much to the consternation of Bethany's congregation. Through this organization, segments of the community worked together to help others learn English, to get the children off the streets, and even to sponsor a Friday evening dance. When we invited some of our church members as chaperones, a row ensued over whether or not the church should be involved in this affair.

Before long Dudley had a real brush with the political power which held a stranglehold on the neighborhood, and I was partly responsible for this encounter. I had always read a great deal, so I naturally joined the Schenectady-Eastern Parkway Library. I found to my amazement that people regularly jammed that facility, standing shoulder to shoulder, and also that many of the books were stacked on the floor. A little investigation showed that the branch library had 44,000 members and 35,000 books, that the building had had no improvements for twenty years, and that almost nothing had been spent on library facilities in Brooklyn, except at Grand Army Plaza, for about twenty-two years—in spite of constant pleas from residents and the New York City Library Committee.

Inquiries among our Jewish friends revealed a readiness for action to seek a change in the library situation, so we organized a Committee for the Extension of Library Facilities in Brooklyn. The Jewish people rallied with great delight around this young Protestant minister and his wife.

The borough president evidenced little interest in this idea, but members of the committee visited his office week after week—on this and other matters. Finally, however, we decided the only way to get action was to obtain petitions. Over one hundred people volunteered to walk up and down those tenement stairs collecting signatures on the petitions. Soon we had basketsful.

When the news of our work got around, Dudley received an invitation, with the committee, to become a spokesman for the New York Library Committee and to represent the Protestant churches of the Borough of Brooklyn. Obviously the library committee had presented dull, repetitious statements before the Board of Estimate over the past years and had accomplished little of significance.

Dudley received a prepared speech to read to the Board of Estimate, chaired by the late Mayor O'Dwyer and including the borough president whom our committee members had hounded. Dudley decided to discard the speech and, with the

31

aid of the committee members, carried the baskets of petitions to the front of the room. There they dropped the baskets in front of the rail. To awaken O'Dwyer, who had dozed during the dull statements, Dudley yelled, "Mr. Mayor, I want to say something to you!"

The mayor woke up quickly, put on his glasses, and stuck his pipe back in his mouth. For the next fifteen minutes he heard statistics and information that he evidently had never heard before.

"Mr. Mayor," Dudley began, "do you realize what's in these baskets? They contain the only thing really important to you—votes!"

For the first time in his life—but not the last—my husband made a headline. Within two years Brooklyn had seven storefront libraries and the Schenectady Avenue branch was expanded.

The experience taught us that power, pressure, people, petitions, and demonstrations are effective tools to use in achieving social and political objectives. Many incidents such as this one occurred during our exciting years in Brooklyn. Although the congregation did not fully understand or agree with Dudley's activism, the Swedish people had a great respect for their pastor and delighted in having a student and his family there to minister to them.

Since the church had no staff, I took any calls that came in during the day while Dudley attended classes at the seminary. Frequently the caller asked for immediate help, so I would put Beverly in her carriage and, with Dianne walking beside it, set off through the streets to find the address. Many times I climbed up or down the endless stairs with the baby in my arms and Dianne trudging along behind. I seldom knew what problem awaited the young minister's wife—a lonely person needing someone to talk to, a mother with a sick child, a desperate woman wanting to talk about her shattering marriage, a shut-in needing assistance.

Sometimes I confronted the tragic side of life as I got someone to remain with the children in another room while I went into the room of a sick person and held the hand of a sufferer. Frequently I prayed or repeated the twenty-third psalm.

Occasionally I went to a family after a loved one had died to console and help and advise. Sometimes I arrived as the person was in the throes of death, and I tried to remain calm in the midst of agony and emotional turmoil. I even straightened out the arms and legs of the deceased person or closed the staring eyes.

During our ministry in Brooklyn, Dudley and I had our first encounters with terminal illness. When we learned that the father and husband of a fine Scottish family had a terminal illness—eighteen months of struggle, pain, operations, and hospitalization—we became involved in helping him and the family. However, the family constantly requested that we did not at any time intimate to this man that he had an incurable disease. This limited our ministry, made it very difficult, and caused the family to misrepresent the facts. I was by the man's bedside in their apartment when death finally came.

Somehow Dudley and I felt cheated and incomplete in our ministry. We almost had a sense of guilt because we had not ignored the family's restriction and told the man of his condition—which he undoubtedly suspected. We felt we could have helped him gain hope and stability and a way to enter death, another experience in the wholeness of life. This memory has remained with us as we have developed a ministry of prayer and health.

The entire pastorate in Brooklyn offered to Dudley and me tremendously meaningful experiences which gave us direction. Those experiences changed my husband's conceptions about the ministry, about the church, as he realized that one of the exciting parts of the ministry is involvement in the lives of people in their social dimensions. What a great exhilaration to see some occasional response, development, rehabilitation of persons—which meant that a spiritual power had really gripped their lives!

The second year of our stay in Brooklyn, dramatic events moved our ministry in another direction as Dudley became determined to attend the First Assembly of the World Council of Churches in Amsterdam, Holland. After (rather brazenly) confronting Bishop G. Bromley Oxnam at an annual conference session with a proposal that he serve as an aide to the bishop at the meeting, Dudley got the desired approval and received a gift of $1,000 from his former business associate to pay for the trip. Great excitement filled our house over plans and preparations for this experience.

That summer while Dudley was in Europe, I took the children for a visit with my family in Canada, then returned to the hot streets of Brooklyn. The strain of those years in the slums had begun to damage my health, and during these weeks my physical condition worsened. One afternoon my doctor told me that I must have immediate surgery and instructed me to sign in at the Methodist Hospital by five o'clock that day.

I knew that Dudley had just left Southampton to return to the United States. I phoned a friend who promised that within a few days she could come to care for the two girls. Leaving them for a time with the sexton and his wife, I traveled by subway to the hospital, signed the register, and faced the uncertainty of those next hours and days after emergency surgery. Because of my poor health, normal healing did not occur, and a few days after Dudley arrived, the entire operation had to be redone, involving intense suffering. Afterward, my strength returned slowly with the demands of school, church, and family.

During my recuperation I had ample time to reflect on the

change that had occurred in my life throughout this Brooklyn pastorate. Before marriage, when I worked in the business world, I had taken great pride in my personal appearance and dress. Though I had lovely things when married, they soon became worn after several years and our budget permitted little replenishing. Fortunately I could sew, and by careful shopping for materials, I made the children's clothing, and sometimes a dress for myself.

Then in Brooklyn I had a new and somewhat shattering experience as parishioners offered me their castoffs. How I struggled with my pride! Other young women in the church dressed smartly. Though I didn't consciously envy them or their lives, I felt inwardly threatened when I observed my husband's admiration for and interest in them. I didn't want to look like the stereotype of "preacher's wife," and I resented that in spite of myself this was happening to me. Caught between two images, I felt threatened by both of them.

I did not feel free to talk with Dudley about this because I was ashamed of my conflicts, so I hid them deep within myself. I knew he could earn a good salary and provide any of my material desires, but I also knew that a complaint would indicate to him that I felt dissatisfied with our life and calling. Furthermore I realized that Christian values aren't automatically acquired when a person decides to dedicate his life to the service of the church. Besides these inner conflicts, I was often physically and mentally exhausted by the demands of the parish and the constant typing of Dudley's course work.

Although I didn't question my love for my husband, I realized that he was ambitious, egotistical, and that he had entered the ministry with gifts that would make a top executive. Lacking financial security, emotional security became increasingly important in my life. Often I misinterpreted Dudley's gregariousness and permitted mental images to form in my mind that created an insecurity which I have never completely erased.

Probably if I could have laughed at my immature reactions or felt free to talk about them with an understanding friend, I would have achieved the proper perspective. Unable to act normally about these fears, I strove harder to maintain the image of the perfect minister's wife.

"We are glad you aren't jealous of your husband," one church member commented.

"I'm just thankful she doesn't show it," another retorted.

When a group of young mothers from our church met for coffee once a week, they explained to me that, though they would like to invite me, they couldn't because this was the time when they "let their hair down" about their husbands, families, and neighborhood events, but they could not extend this freedom to me. They had to maintain a certain image about their pastor, so I couldn't join their group and talk about him. It took me several years to feel grateful for this exclusion and to see it as a discipline, something to pray about.

Two occurrences during my illness in Brooklyn nourished me. The Brooklyn air carried dirt, a lot of it, filtering through the window sills, doors, and every crack, bringing to the housekeeper the unpleasant task of trying to keep ahead of its relentless spread. During my illness and recuperation I worried because I could not keep the house as clean as I had before. One day the doorbell rang. Answering it, I was surprised to see one of our church women, who cleaned houses each day to support her family, standing there with several bars of soap. She had personally made the soap and had come to scrub my floors. I still remember the strength of her arms and the joy she showed in performing this service.

Another time a woman of questionable character came with a bottle of cologne. She had sacrificed to buy this, so I used it carefully because I felt it represented something lovely about her womanhood. In Brooklyn I had many personal glimpses of the real persons behind the facades or the reputations they had acquired.

Some time after Dudley returned from the World Council of Churches meeting in Europe, he was offered, and accepted, the directorship of the Study of the Ethics and Economics of Society financed by the Rockefeller Foundation and sponsored by the Federal Council of Churches, later the National Council of Churches. Now his ministry underwent another radical change.

In the summer of 1950 we moved from the teeming inner city to Oceanside, Long Island, where Dudley served as interim pastor at the Methodist church. One day after we had moved into the parsonage there, Dianne rushed up to me, buried her head in my lap, and exclaimed, "Oh, Mother, we have come home!"

When I asked what she meant, she replied, "The windows. This house has windows all the way around it!"

The crowded city life for the past three years had not deadened the child's recollection of the first house in the hills of Delaware.

In August we moved again, to Roosevelt, Long Island, into our own home, on which we paid off the mortgage in three years. Here less than a year after we moved in I experienced the critical operation for removal of the massive growths and the fetus of our third child. Two years from the time we purchased this home our son, John, was born.

For the first time since Dudley had decided to enter the ministry, we had no direct involvement with a local congregation. That, however, did not last long. In the fall Dudley was appointed to begin a new church, the first new congregation established in the New York East Conference in fifty-two years, in the town of Merrick. For a year and a half the fledgling congregation met in the local fire hall.

Dudley thought it was great to go on Sunday mornings to

open the windows, clean up the floors, set up chairs amid the aroma of beer and tobacco, which had set the tone of the usual Saturday night parties.

"This really gives our church an existential beginning," Dudley used to joke.

We both relished the adventure of building a new congregation. People began to come—all kinds of people, from the big city, from overseas, recent army dischargees. Those who came from larger churches soon saw that they would not dominate this new congregation, because those persons new to church life clearly indicated that they would resist conformity to old patterns. Dudley talked excitedly to me about this completely experimental setting into which God placed us.

Merrick, a new, clean suburban community, would, we assumed, harbor none of the starkness of life which we experienced in downtown Brooklyn. I recall one of my enthusiastic husband's first sermons.

"It's really great to be in such a location," he told the congregation, "because having come from the burdens of a downtown parish, we feel we've moved into a clean, problem-free area. Here we'll be involved in a ministry of a different nature, one uncluttered by the demands of both social and personal problems which resulted from life in the big city."

A year later he preached another sermon in the fire hall sanctuary.

"You may recall that one year ago I said we were grateful for the opportunity to preach and work in a clean, problem-free community, uncluttered by the problems and demands of big city life. Well, in this one year I have learned that I made an almost entirely wrong assumption. That kind of freedom does not exist."

People who came from Brooklyn, Manhattan, and other cities across the nation did not leave their human problems behind. Here we experienced anti-Catholicism, anti-Protestant-

38

ism, and anti-Semitism in its rawest form, as high school youth from some of the community's finest families were arrested for destroying the lawns of Jewish families by driving through them. Dudley sensed this same anti-Semitism among leading members of our congregation and worked to help these persons overcome this prejudice which prevented brotherhood in its real sense to pervade the community.

Here also a new god had risen among lower-middle-class America, the postwar development home with its expansion attic. Each person slaved to obtain all of the space and gadgets offered by our affluent society. Dudley had a real problem convincing the young men, and some older ones also, that they should put aside their building, planting, repairing, and other home work to attend worship or participate in the life of the church.

Early in this ministry, Dudley urged the congregation to participate in community activities, a brotherhood council, the school board, citizenship clubs, and county political organizations. In a short time members held key spots within some of these organizations, and several played important roles in the initiation of a brotherhood council.

Besides the community involvement, my experimenting husband soon began study courses in theology, church history, Bible, and ethics—which naturally gave him the chance to relate his ministry to the Rockefeller Foundation Study Project as group participants began to share some of their vocational problems.

Dealing with the power struggle between cliques within the church became one of the young pastor's major worries. I watched him developing new understanding of the sharp differences among people and smiled inwardly as he used a firmness I had not seen before. This struggle intensified as the congregation began to plan for a building. Some wanted to erect an educational plant first, but Dudley became con-

39

vinced that we needed a sanctuary with as many educational rooms as possible. During the period of discussion and planning, our home became the headquarters, which, I must admit, caused certain tensions as the members intruded into our family life.

Anyone who thinks "knock-down, drag-out fights" aren't possible within the Christian community should have been around during the planning stages of this building project. The president of the WSCS and the church treasurer—husband and wife—lined up other members to oppose the plans developing under Dudley's leadership. One evening in an official board meeting, the treasurer strongly opposed one of Dudley's positions. When he did not get the support he expected, he angrily offered his resignation, which Dudley promptly accepted. Greatly surprised, the treasurer left the meeting with his wife. Before noon the next day, the district superintendent visited our house. He was obviously upset because the treasurer and his wife had come from one of the largest churches in Brooklyn. Dudley, however, stuck to his decision; the congregation pulled itself together and moved ahead.

"A time comes when a break is the best thing that can happen," Dudley said to me one evening as we talked over these events. "Handled with understanding, but firmness, it can lead to good."

During the church's construction, much of it done by the men of the church, another problem arose. One Friday afternoon in December the beautiful West Coast fir trusses arrived at the railway siding. A truck brought them, together with thousands of feet of planking for the roof, beams, and exposed planked ceiling. Weather reports indicated a change over the weekend from good to bad, which meant that unless the workers protected the trusses and planking with a special stain, the wood would get wet and damaged. The men of the church met Friday night and, after discussion, decided to work all weekend—including Sunday—to stain the wood. They did, however, suggest that the pastor do some parish visiting Sunday afternoon rather than join in the painting.

The congregation received some criticism for this Sunday labor. However, it helped the people see that facing responsibilities sometimes calls for modification of legalisms or traditional positions. On Easter Sunday in 1953 the men worked until almost five o'clock in the morning to erect the last pew, lay the final asphalt tile, and finish the necessary painting. In less than three years this congregation, through vital lay direction and part-time ministerial help, had grown to a membership of five hundred and built a new building. Instead of inviting some dignitary to speak at the first service in the new building, the congregation wanted its own minister to preach and its laymen to participate in the service, indicating a recognition of the responsibilities members of this church would face together.

During the Merrick ministry, I felt the need for further understanding of the Christian faith and the place of the minister in the church, and decided to obtain a local preacher's license through the conference course of studies. I did this and found that my achievement impressed several laymen in the church. They also began to consider the study leading to ordination. After a time several laymen of our congregation did complete the course and decided to retire early in order to serve in the church.

Toward the close of our third year in this pastorate, Dudley and I began to realize that we again would soon face a vocational decision. We thought about settling with this congregation and enjoying the work here for a number of years. Dudley, however, expressed an acute sensitivity to the rising problems of race, international affairs, and extremism. Thus, I wondered and prayed about our future, knowing that we both believed God would reveal his will for us.

41

In May of 1953 a new door opened when Dudley received an invitation to become the first executive secretary of the newly organized Board of Social and Economic Relations of The Methodist Church, with headquarters in Chicago. He accepted, and we prepared for the transition from this loving local experience to the mainstream of institutional agency life in the church.

Arriving in November, 1953, on the North Shore of Chicago, we suddenly realized that this new work would mean a complete reorganization of family and personal life. While Dudley would have national and international contacts in his work, his family would become just another family living on a street. That Christmas our oldest daughter, Dianne, remembers having an empty kind of feeling as she realized she was no longer a parish minister's daughter on whom the congregation showered gifts.

We faced other startling realizations. After we sat together as a family in the local church and listened to the sermon, which was quite good, Dudley came away asking, "Do I really have to believe all that stuff I heard and have spoken myself for such a long time?" Obviously he felt different in the pew than he did in the pulpit. We also had to adjust to new relationships with the people of the community. For a change, we had to create relationships now that we were not a parsonage family. Both Dudley and I soon decided that being placed superficially on a pedestal or receiving reverence because of his position were not the best credentials for acceptance into the real dynamics of community life. In fact, being a ministerial family sometimes excluded us from genuinely entering community and social life—particularly in a community where the people didn't generally hold to social patterns which paralleled those of Methodism.

As Dudley began this new social action venture, the children and I saw little of him. After a time, however, he slowed down his seven-day-week schedule and gave a higher priority to his family life. Our new home needed a lot of renovation, so we spent spare hours fixing up the kitchen, building a family room, extending the house to provide a new bedroom and bath for the girls. We also created a lovely garden, which helped us to make many new friends in the neighborhood as persons came to admire and obtain our flowers.

In the new community we also became involved in the public school, where my husband and I worked hard to begin foreign language instruction in the lower grades. Now that we had become lay members of a local church instead of pastor and wife, we had to serve there differently also, so Dudley and I worked in the adult department, developing a new plan of adult study.

We had always made Bible study and devotions a vital part of our lives. In the early years of our marriage, Dudley and I had devotions together, and as the children came, they became a natural part of our spiritual disciplines. They shared often by reading the Bible or writing little prayers.

Now, however, with Dudley away three-quarters of the time, I faced a new challenge and tried several methods which failed—even tested procedures described in various books. Finally, I decided that dinner time, when we all sat together around the table, would be best. I would ask the children to come early to the table, read something from the Bible, and then join hands in prayer for our home, family, and their father—so he was in a sense included with us at the table.

Dianne, the eldest, naturally rebelled first against this discipline. She began to bring a book with her to the table; she put it on her lap and refused to listen to the devotions. At prayer time she joined in the handclasp, but kept on reading her book. One night she couldn't stand it any longer, jumped up, slammed her book on the table and said impatiently: "Mother, why don't you stop trying to act like the father? When you try to be the father, I hate you, but when you're the mother, I love you. When you're both mother and father, I don't get you at all."

That ended my attempts to have family worship with the young children. I waited until Dudley came home, recognizing that he was head of the home and that we really couldn't have family devotions without the whole family. When home, he led the worship and we all joined in.

I did not stop working to provide a home atmosphere of prayer though, because I realized that, as a mother, I had a daily responsibility to provide a spirit of worship. I had to provide the spirit of prayer within the home just as I had to have clean clothes for the children, well-balanced meals, sanitary bedrooms, and all the other important things in children's growth.

As my husband and I look back to these years, we see that our search had taken several directions. Both he and I had to adjust to a new kind of work within the church. We also had to reorganize our family life around lay participation in church and community. The children and I had to adjust to Dudley's demanding travel schedule which caused disruptions and often dissatisfaction in our home. Both he and I realized, though, that we should concentrate on development of family life, especially in relationship to prayer, devotional experience, and the spiritual growth of our children. Thus we worked to strengthen our prayer life. At this time we didn't know what lay ahead of us and how our devotional disciplines would undergird us.

4 | LIGHT IN THE DARK VALLEY OF SUFFERING

I stood with my guide at the completion of a tour of the Hermitage in Leningrad. We had come to Europe during 1958, when Dudley attended the Theological Institute at Oxford. Then we had traveled on to Russia, where we met and talked with many young persons training to become members of the Communist Party. Our guide on this tour frankly admitted her desire to qualify for membership in this organization dedicated to radical social reconstruction.

Feeling weary, I requested permission to return to our hotel, but this tall young woman urged, "Please do not go yet. There is something you must see. It is the most beautiful thing in all of my country that I can show you!" Sensitive to my tiredness, she offered to take me ahead of the others so we could see this wonder together.

We walked down the street to another building, which had served as a palace of the czars—a strange couple, this American minister's wife and her young Communist hopeful. During the tour she and I had walked ahead of the group. She told me of her great country and its leaders and I talked of mine. But often

I found myself talking to her about the central person of my life, Jesus Christ.

As we walked on, I wondered about this thing of beauty which she wanted to show me. At a gateway we climbed a wide, white marble stairway, made a sharp turn, and suddenly faced a great iridescent painting. In the silence of this onetime Russian palace I heard a sigh, and looking around, I saw tears running down my guide's face.

"It is Jesus healing Jairus' daughter," she whispered.

I knew then that underneath all those layers of Communist training this girl held a memory from a young age, a memory of her introduction to Jesus, and she wanted to share it with me. A light shone from the painting, and I heard a voice in the thundering silence.

"Alice Ward, do you know the healing Jesus?"

I could not escape the voice and the question it asked. Mentally I began to reply. Surely this was the Christ I had seen in my mother as she ministered to the sick in our home and in that Canadian village. This same Christ compelled a minister to leave his bed on a cold winter's night and walk along icy streets to stand for a moment beside my hospital bed, to take my hand and say simply, "I had to come." Only Christ could have transformed the pain of those hours, removed the fears, and guided the hands of the surgeon in the morning. The same Jesus made it possible for me to again know the joy of health and the miracle of my son's birth.

Still the question persisted in spite of my answers. I searched the Scriptures, rethought our calling and work, studied teaching and preaching. Had we truly fulfilled Christ's command to teach, to preach, and to heal? Had I taken my healing to others? How much was I personally involved in their suffering for total healing? Passionately I sought to find this Jesus, this Christ who ministers to the whole of man. Little did I know the pain and suffering, the struggle of body, mind, and soul, which I would soon suffer.

One day before Christmas of 1958 I went to my doctor for a thorough, routine examination which indicated that I was in good health. Some days later, Dudley left on a lengthy trip. That night I had finished my work and gone to bed, lying comfortably on the bedclothes to read while the girls completed their homework. Turning one page of the book, my hand rested on my left breast. Suddenly it seemed as though the light went out of my world.

Cold fear swept over me as I felt a lump under my hand. This time the gift of perception which I had had since childhood did not spare me. That day I had received a letter from my doctor confirming the excellent reports of the examination. I knew that no more similar letters would arrive. I peered into my future, not a morbid person looking fatalistically at something dreadful, but a realistic person facing something I could not escape.

That night I had to decide how to face this new fact of my life. The girls came to say goodnight and returned to their rooms, not knowing that for their mother this would be the dark night of her soul. I knew a dimension of aloneness there in my bedroom that I had never experienced before. I thought of Dudley as he went on another mission for the church, and I wondered if somehow we had missed the very core of the gospel for which we worked so hard. I thought of my church that I loved, of the many fine people in its midst, but somehow it seemed dark and cold as I lay on my pillow.

Though I tried hard, I could think of no power to meet my need. We belonged to no prayer group, and I could think of no one at that moment whom I could phone to relieve my own disturbance, fear, and anxiety with their strength. I had not yet discovered the Jesus whom I had sought since that day in Russia months ago. Would He really be a part of my suffering, or would I be at the mercy of medical science and technology?

How I agonized that night—about Christmas, the children, our many plans for the family. With my mind occupied with the many things I felt I had to solve as a mother, I could not pray for myself. I knew that the lump I felt had grown in my physical body, but how does a person pray for herself when she's searching and becomes physically and mentally involved? Should I pray to escape the whole adventure, or was I willing to become part of it even though it may mean pain and suffering? Should I pray at all? Was this ordeal to be part of my search, part of my discovery of the healing Jesus?

I kept my fearful secret locked within myself for several days before I told Dudley and then called my doctor to schedule another appointment. He advised surgery, but suggested I wait until after Christmas and then have the operation as soon as possible. Dudley and I decided to share the news with no one in our family during the holiday season because, frankly, we did not want others adding to our own anxiety and fears. So we had our Christmas celebration and all its involvements— visits, parties for the children, and multiple religious activities.

Immediately after the first of the year I entered Wesley Memorial Hospital in Chicago. The impending surgery did not particularly disturb me, since the doctors and surgeons indicated that they expected nothing unusual. Still, Dudley and I recognized that in such times persons must prepare for the unpredictable and understand that many cases prove more drastic than anticipated.

On the afternoon before surgery a team of medical men, including the man recognized as the most able soft tissue surgeon in the Chicago area, gave their judgment that the tumor would be benign and easily excised and that all should go well. They estimated two hours for time in surgery.

As I looked out the window from my hospital bed, I knew that if I did not look out at the same sight—the magnificent Drake Hotel—until the same time tomorrow, I would have had radical surgery for breast cancer. If the operation were a simple one, I would be out of surgery in less than an hour. I thought of the many times that Dudley had sat with parishioners as they also waited for the results of an operation.

The possibility of having a breast removed terrifies a woman because her breasts symbolize her life and womanhood. The operation can also severely shock a husband who is proud of his wife and her appearance. The night before the surgery I put my hand on this breast and thanked God for it. I thanked him for this creation of beauty, for the wonderful time when, as a young girl, I realized that I could now buy a brassiere, that I approached womanhood. I recalled the times in our marriage when Dudley had kidded me about my full, good figure. I remembered, too, his pride in my appearance. I thanked God for the joy of nursing my babies and seeing them grow strong and healthy. Now I faced the possibility of losing this symbol of my womanhood, and I wondered how I would react if my breast were really removed.

Dudley and I prepared for the next day with hope, but also with the awareness that the report might not be good. We carefully examined our response to bad news and determined to face the issue directly, to share it and face it immediately with honesty and candor, not attempting to shield anything from each other. We also decided to take the children into our confidence whatever the outcome.

Early in the morning of the surgery, Dudley came to the hospital. Together we committed ourselves to God and to the medical care in which we had great confidence. After attendants took me into the operating room, Dudley waited as do all relatives of persons in surgery. When I remained in surgery for a longer period of time than expected, he began to suspect that the operation had not gone as well as the doctors predicted.

About three o'clock in the afternoon, Dudley discovered that I had just then been placed in the recovery room and that the doctors had performed a very difficult operation.

In a short time the hospital chaplain came to talk with my anxious husband. A good man, accustomed to dealing with nonministerial patients and relatives, the chaplain came with the usual shibboleths and trite statements, concerned, but inadequately prepared for this kind of situation.

"Thanks for trying," Dudley said after the chaplain had spoken, "but what you've said doesn't help me at all. I've said the same things often to many persons facing the same situation I'm facing. Perhaps some were helped by my words, but they aren't much help in this kind of a crisis."

Dudley's words shocked the chaplain; perhaps they began some rethinking on his part. However, many experiences since have confirmed for us the belief that much preparation of the minister for counseling, visiting, comforting, strengthening people in emotional and physical crises is almost useless and perhaps could better be discarded.

For the next two hours Dudley sat quietly, anxiously, until he could talk with the surgeons. About five o'clock the chief surgeon, Dr. Peter Rosi, came to see him. He explained that he had been so busy after the operation that he could not come down immediately. As the doctor began, Dudley asked him to speak frankly.

"Everything went well at first. The initial stages of the operation validated my prognosis. Then, when we were just about ready to close up, I discovered a mass which did not show up on any of the tests. It was very deeply embedded. I tried my best to get all the growth from the immediate area and I think I succeeded. But then I decided to do a complete mastectomy.

You know that involves the neck, arm, and some areas in the back. It was necessary."

Dr. Rosi and Dudley talked about the convalescence and the necessary procedures to assure my recovery. The doctor advised, and Dudley agreed, that if things went normally, I should have extensive cobalt treatments as a preventative measure as soon as possible.

At about six o'clock the attendants took me back to my room where equipment, instruments, pumps, intravenous stands and bottles, blood, and special nursing care awaited the patient. At about seven I mumbled a few words to Dudley. As soon as my consciousness began to return, I knew instinctively that I had had radical surgery. My breast was gone!

"I have cancer."

"Yes, and that means we face a new situation, but we agreed to confront it together, and we will."

Toward the middle of the evening, Dr. Rosi, now in a business suit, came to the room and took time, as we requested, to give Dudley and me a professional explanation of what the operation really involved. He did this in an attitude of deep concern and compassion. Throughout his explanation he held my hand in a quiet, yet firm, support.

"The second growth was malignant and that required massive surgery. You lost one breast completely, Alice, and I had to remove the nerves and lymph glands of your back, neck, and arm. This means you'll need a lot of extensive therapy, a program of exercise and stimulation. As I pointed out to Dudley earlier, you ought to begin cobalt therapy also as a preventative measure. That also ought to take care of any possible immediate spread of the malignancy which I couldn't get to in surgery."

As Dr. Rosi talked with us, we realized the great difference between a person who acts out of high professional competence and genuine spiritual understanding and the person who reacts out of goodwill and role playing.

These initial events set a pattern for our reaction throughout the ordeal and helped us to find the positive values which emerged and continued to emerge as we faced crises many times since this one. During this period certain new realizations began to confront Dudley. As he waited many hours while I endured my cobalt treatments, or as he made contacts in work or in social activities, he realized that when other couples faced a similar situation, the husband frequently developed a repulsion toward the entire ordeal, a disgust compounded by fright and apprehension for the future. The radical change in a wife's personal appearance can cause this feeling, which can grow into a point of real distress and tension. Hysterectomies, performed for preventative reasons following a mastectomy, often aggravate the problem because the woman feels deprived of her figure and of her feminine completeness, including her reproductive capacity. Thus she faces a period of hazard in her emotional, particularly sexual, adjustment, and this can nearly ruin a marriage.

"I began to realize," Dudley told me later, "that unless I could deal directly with these apprehensions which are so characteristic and which have harmed the relationship between husband and wife, I would run into the same problems as others with whom I had spoken.

"As I thought about this, I remembered one of the early assumptions about a man's relationship to a woman. The ultimate happiness for a man comes in the complete happiness of the woman. It was easy to see this as a fundamental principle in sexual relationships, but now I had to experience it on a different level if you and I were to meet, wholesomely, without regret, the sense of challenge in this new experience.

"So I began a search for the meaning of crisis, for a rational approach to the problems and a recognition of the incompleteness of our trite religious assumptions and resources. Eventually I came to the conclusion that unless I could personally incorporate into this experience spiritual guidance directly from God, I probably wouldn't be any different from other persons, with or without religion. As a person with physical and emotional needs and as a spiritual being, I needed to see these aspects come together in an integrated relationship."

Dudley admitted that this did not come easily at first, especially during the period of terribly uncomfortable recuperation, made more difficult by the burning and bleeding from the cobalt treatments. This all required everything he could muster to achieve the physical, emotional, and spiritual integration he sought, and it began a new search. During this period, Dudley expressed great skepticism about his spiritual resources and those offered by the church. He had not yet experienced a new awareness which was to emerge in him of new dimensions of spiritual vitality and strength. He realized, however, that in a practical way professional persons, such as Dr. Rosi, the radio therapist, and others on the hospital staff, could become positive examples in his search.

"At this point my appreciation of the meaning of prayer in healing began to take form," Dudley told me.

Shortly after the surgery, the question arose as to whether or not Dudley should keep a speaking engagement at Central Methodist Church in Pheonix, Arizona. Wrestling with the question, Dudley delayed making a travel reservation until the Saturday afternoon before. Then he found that a strike had shut down American Airlines, and TWA, the only other line to Phoenix, had no openings. After calling a friend, a vice-president of the airline, Dudley decided that if a seat opened up and if I felt up to his absence, he would go.

Saturday afternoon the seat did become available, but as Dudley walked into my room, I spoke before he had a chance to say a word.

"Dudley, I'm telling you, you must go to preach tomorrow. It will be the beginning of freedom in your work."

My husband arrived in Phoenix at sunset, registered at a lovely motel, and enjoyed a swim. During the night he awakened several times to think about the critical situation.

"Why should I be in Phoenix and not in Chicago?"

In the morning Dudley wrestled with another question: Should he call the hospital? He knew that if he called and learned that I had weakened, his preaching would be affected.

"I had a deep sense that a crisis had come up during the night," Dudley later reported. "Finally I decided to risk upsetting my preaching, and I called Chicago. I got through to the nursing station where they told me that you couldn't take calls, but they told me to hold the line while they went to see whether or not the doctors or nurses were in the room. Fortunately both the doctor and nurse were in the room. The doctor told me that things looked a little better this morning and then said, 'I believe I'll hold the phone to her ear and mouth so that you can talk to her.'"

When the doctor placed that phone by my face, I told Dudley that I had become weak during the night and needed medical attention. During that time, I called out to God for a lifeline, which didn't come immediately, but I got my answer in the morning. The telephone rang during a period when I was alone in the room. That was strange, because all calls to this room were blocked. Though I wasn't supposed to move, I could reach the phone this time and I maneuvered just enough to get the receiver and put it to my ear.

"Mrs. Ward, I have been praying for you and I wanted to call you. I had to tell you this morning somehow or other."

The lifeline I needed had arrived. The voice on the phone belonged to Bishop Matthew W. Clair, Jr., one of Methodism's distinguished black bishops. During the short conversation, in which he shared his concern and affection, he indicated more completely than any other person had ever done the depth of communion which can take place spiritually across all kinds ot barriers.

Dudley and I knew that God had answered our prayers and that this day would be a good one for us both.

"You stay there and preach," I told Dudley, "and invite the entire congregation to pray for me."

That Sunday congregations in both services of this church offered special prayers for me.

Dudley and I had prayed together the first night after surgery while he remained with me the whole night, and, with the help of a general nurse, took care of my needs. In the midst of my pain, we prayed and talked about the future days. As we prepared for the night together, Dudley called T. Otto Nall, editor of the *Christian Advocate,* and now a bishop.

"Otto, we are in the midst of a crisis and I want to stay here all night. Would you mind going to the house and sleeping there to look after the children?"

Then Dudley called our children and told them that Dr. Nall would stay with them that night because he needed to be with me. Dudley and I agreed that he should go home early in the morning to be with the children when they woke up.

The next morning Dudley arrived home before seven, made orange juice for the children, and then wakened them to talk about the serious health problems I faced. The three children and their father sat on one of the beds and faced the situation with some apprehension, of course, but without any hysteria. Thus the children became part of the decisions we made during this crisis period.

On another occasion during the hospitalization, when my husband had stayed most of the night, we shared an experience together which has guided us greatly all the years since. In the midst of intense pain and weakness, I saw death's door open, ever so clearly. It was set in a beautiful soft blue light with clear, vibrant, lively colors in the approach to the door, the entrance itself, and beyond. I wished desperately to go through, for it was obviously so inviting and easy to enter into that new experience.

As I moved toward the door, the Lord himself appeared in the entrance in beauty, love, and majesty. He said, "I know you would like to come, but this is not the time. I want you to go back into earth's consciousness. I have a mission for you to perform, and when it is completed, you may come with a wonderful welcome."

The Lord knew what was best, and has provided the health, energy, and spiritual vitality to me for the best ten years of work, service, and pure pleasure of my entire life.

Dudley had difficulty finding help to care for the children and our home, but somehow my family managed. During the many weeks of my recuperation, the "sophisticates" of the North Shore of Chicago, those people who supposedly valued isolation and avoided involvement with others, banded together to help us. They offered to have us eat our evening meals in their homes. When we decided to avoid the disruption which this would bring to our family, the neighbors provided a full meal for our table each evening. This kind of concern and involvement showed us again the innate compassion of one human being for another.

Our friends and neighbors also cooperated to get me to the hospital each day for many weeks. They made the trip of a dozen miles during those winter months filled with ice and snow and cold weather. On particularly bad days, one of the members of our church, a Red Cross driver, made the trip in her station wagon.

In those months following the surgery, though they were filled with many difficulties, Dudley canceled no speaking engagements, kept his office schedule, and even went to Honolulu to direct the first social action conference in the

Hawaiian Methodist Mission and to participate in Religious Emphasis Week at the University of Hawaii. Some colleagues, neighbors, and friends could not understand why he continued this routine when I was so gravely ill, but both he and I are glad that he continued his work. I could have become an easy reason for him to remain at home or to let work responsibilities slide. Instead, he strengthened his resources during this period.

As Dudley and I thought about the criticism, we realized that many persons tend to identify with disaster and crisis in a negative rather than a positive way. However, very positive benefits frequently emerge from tragedy. Persons must realize that physical and emotional crises are part of the whole context of life. How could I have genuine emotional and physical healing unless Dudley had freedom in his search for reality and to carry out his responsibilities? How proud I was when Dudley penned this meaningful dedicatory statement in his 1961 book on the Social Creed:

> *To my wife, Alice*
> *who has demonstrated by her life*
> *that personal religious experience and*
> *vital social concern belong together*

Dudley and I shared another realization during this period, especially during the daily cobalt treatment: the church is inadequate in such situations; even the ministerial services in the hospital cannot give constructive, positive emotional and spiritual care for the persons going through the therapy process.

The cobalt room was the loneliest place that Dudley and I had ever been, a place forcing people to face the hard facts of life, a place frequently stimulating shock and hysteria. Not once during the entire period of my cobalt treatment did any minister or even the chaplain of the hospital visit the clinic. The person experiences the cobalt treatment completely alone, isolated from all contacts, even doctors and nurses. The patients wait alone, go through the treatment alone, and come out of it alone facing a period of immediate adjustment. This experience helped my minister-husband and me to see the need to develop insights which might help other people facing such crises.

During this entire experience I marveled at the mature insights and reactions of the children, who participated on every level of the crisis. Naturally they became disturbed at times. Afternoon after afternoon John would come home to find a different person to look after him. Occasionally he wandered aimlessly back to school and said to the teacher who questioned his after-hours presence there, "I wasn't sure where I was to go after school today." Even he, however, had little noticeable distress.

John's sensitivity to the situation showed the first day I could go to his classroom for one of the parent-children parties. Each mother sat in a chair beside the desk of her child. John, I learned, had always sat beside the teacher's desk during the past months. When the room was all arranged for this party, John looked up, smiled, and said, "Now everyone has a mother."

Magnificent in their response, the girls quickly began to mature, to think for themselves about my illness, and to join in many talks about our family's situation. As Dianne, our oldest daughter, completed her application for entrance to a university, she came to the questions on health.

"Daddy," she asked, "should I put down the word—cancer?"

"What do you want to do?" Dudley responded.

"Yes, we have all faced Mother's disease and should be honest," she decided.

A deep faith inspired the spirit that prevailed in our home during those difficult months. The joy of childhood and youth

58

contributed to that mood. Often in the morning I would hear Johnny calling out, "Mother, come here quickly!" Struggling out of bed after a long night of intense suffering, I would go into his room.

"Look, Mother, look at the beautiful star that is still in the sky!"

As Johnny and I sat on his bed and looked out the window, I caught the hope and beauty of both the child and God's universe which amazed the child. Each morning during all those weeks of recuperation I got up early, prepared my children's breakfast, talked with them, and helped them get ready for school. I think they never left home feeling anxious about leaving me. In their youthful way, they understood the strength within me, a strength that transcended anything physical. Without that strength I could not have endured this period of hardship.

I thought I had known something about aloneness, especially as Dudley's work changed and he spent so much time away from his family. Many evenings I had put the children to bed and sat alone. But I never faced an aloneness such as that of the cobalt room.

That first day as Dudley helped me undress and put on the surgical gown, I whispered to him, "Please say the twenty-third psalm for me." To prepare for this unknown experience I determined to think about that psalm and not become afraid. He repeated the psalm for me and, like a child, I said it after him.

Then my turn came and attendants ushered me into the cobalt room, bare except for the massive machinery and movable slab on which I would lie. The attendants wheeled the slab underneath the imposing machinery, removed the gown, and placed a sheet over my body. Lead protectors placed around the area where the rays would penetrate shielded the surrounding areas.

"Your first treatment will continue for twenty minutes," someone told me. "We will control the machinery from outside. During your treatment time nobody will come into the room and you will not be able to contact anyone. Please lie perfectly still and try not to move any part of your body."

With everything in place, the attendants left the room and closed the door. Someone started the machine. I could hear movement, something like a clock ticking off periods of the treatment. Twenty minutes! That's a short time when you're alive and active. Twenty minutes on a slab in the cobalt room seemed like an eternity.

I tried to recall the twenty-third psalm, but loneliness swept over me as I could not remember one word. In that awful moment of intense aloneness, struggling to obey the command not to move, I felt a desperation I had never before known. I could contact no one, not even God, and I realized something of the meaning of Jesus' cry on the cross: "My God, my God, why hast thou forsaken me?"

Day after day I experienced this desperation in the cobalt room. Dudley would say the twenty-third psalm over and over to me before I went into that room. Earlier I had read it during the evening and at night and in the morning before I left home for the clinic. I would repeat it carefully, making sure that I knew every word. But when the door closed and I lay alone under that whirring machine, I could remember nothing, and I lay utterly and completely alone. Sometimes I wondered: Am I losing my sanity?

Then one day a presence came into the cobalt room. It remained in the farthest corner as though trying to get as far from the condition damaging my physical body as possible. I tried to turn my head to recognize the presence, but could not. Though comforted by this sense of a presence with me, I also felt a rejection of my personal self. God himself stood apart from the cancer, and I, almost in the last hour, had been turned over to science and technology to prevent the spread of the disease threatening my life.

Only the entrance of the attendant to change my position for treating various parts of my body interrupted my time in the cobalt room, now lengthened to nearly one hour. One day I became conscious of more than a presence with me. I heard a voice speaking in the room. Since I could not move my head, I allowed my mind to search the room, trying to identify the place from which the voice came. Days after first hearing the voice I suddenly realized that it sprang from the very center of my being, as though rising up from within me. For the first time in the cobalt room, I heard the words of the twenty-third psalm. I didn't say those words, but rather they came from the voice speaking within me.

"The Lord is."

For many days I would hear these three words during the cobalt treatment. I kept this experience to myself, not even sharing it with Dudley. I didn't want him to know my desperation or to share my fear that in the intensity of the treatment I might be losing the faculty of remembrance. Thus, hearing these three words, I experienced the power of listening and silence.

The Spirit itself, I believe, repeated the twenty-third psalm for me, not all at once, not in any one day, but daily adding to the initial three words the other words of that psalm. With the words came an enlightenment, an inward revelation of the meaning of each line, each phrase, of this strength-providing psalm, as though my parents and Sunday school had taught it to me as a child and I had retained it across the years only to lose that memory in the terror of the cobalt room. Yet God had not left me alone. Instead, he had used this experience to teach me the psalm himself, to teach it to me, not as a little child, but as a woman facing the stark reality of life and death. In the days and years ahead, it would mean life itself to me.

61

This experience began an involvement that would remain with me the rest of my life. I realized that I had to learn the meaning of this psalm in a wider, deeper, and higher dimension. In the moment of my greatest aloneness, the Spirit taught me the twenty-third psalm. I knew at that time, and have reinforced my knowledge in later years, that God does not fear cancer. God is greater than cancer. He holds the ultimate victory. By daily relating to his presence, I, too, can know victory.

5 | THE LIGHT BECOMES BRIGHTER

One morning as I changed the dressing, I felt overwhelmed by the extent of the surgery, the ugliness of the deep burns of therapy, both front and back, and thoughts of the long struggle ahead. I knew that no human being, regardless of color, social or economic status, would change places with me; in truth I stood empty handed with nothing to offer my Lord. I sank to the floor and cried in despair.

In this experience of aloneness, nothingness, and utter defeat, I heard the voice of Christ, and I felt his hands upon my shoulder.

"Because you have nothing to bring, and no one else would claim you, I want you. I will re-create you, I will mold you according to my plan, and I will use you. You must follow the disciplines of the spirit as your entire being is reshaped to become my witness."

No instantaneous miracle followed to heal and perfect my physical body, but as I stood up I received instructions about the first steps in spiritual discipline. To restore the muscles in my left side and arm, I had to exercise a designated time each day. Now I would give the same amount of time to spiritual exercise, silent listening and prayer, both carried out alone in my room. Just as at first I could only exercise the physical body for five-minute periods, the spiritual exercise began in the same limited way. At the beginning it was sheer torture to sit alone on a chair in my room facing myself and God. In the initial stages I used simple exercises, almost childish, relaxing, breathing, becoming aware not of my aloneness, but rather of a Presence.

I found one very effective healing agent in the care of my skin following burns and subsequent scar tissue to be the use of vitamin E. I purchased the large, 100-unit capsules and opened them so that I could apply the vitamin directly to the area, However, when taking it internally, I purchased the smaller, concentrated capsule of vitamin E.

As the periods of physical exercise lengthened, so also did the time of stillness and listening. Before long I understood the interrelatedness of the two forms of exercise, one dependent on the other. Some of the struggle became an adventure. I knew, through the Spirit, that in seeking or asking for physical healing I must also willingly offer up everything that I was for healing, that I must offer for complete healing cancer in all forms known and unknown to my conscious mind. Just as healing for the physical body required time, attention, and all the knowledge of medical science and technology, so the healing of the mind and spirit would require all available help through the Spirit. Willing to receive the one, I must also willingly receive the other. I received no answers to the question: Why? In fact, I felt moved to avoid spending time and energy in search of such answers.

While kind people often offer misguided expressions of concern, I felt directed to restrict visitors who felt sympathy for me. They would drain energy from my body, energy needed in the rebuilding process. During this period I spent little time with people outside my family. I read different books, had

64

opportunities to talk with experienced persons, and thought about new ideas. I also took long walks along the shore of Lake Michigan, and these became times of interaction of the two exercises, one for body, the other for the mind, in communion with the Spirit of God, which I discovered everywhere.

I learned of a service for Communion and healing held once a week in the local Episcopal church. I obtained permission to attend, but could not receive the sacrament. This denial of the sacrament became a discipline that I used as a teaching and blessing over the next two years. The denial of a material thing created aliveness to the Spirit that I had not known before in Communion. After a time I realized that God was using me as a channel for healing to others who came to the service in expectation. In place of resentment at being denied the sacrament, I found an opportunity to pray for others as they knelt to receive the blessing of Communion and the laying-on of hands. On the morning of my last visit to the chapel, I had a rare experience. As I sat in my usual place in the back row, watching the others as they went to the altar rail, the room became filled with light and alive with the Presence. It seemed that Christ himself took the elements from the altar and fed them to me, laying his hands upon my head and giving me the fullness of his blessing.

Dudley had expressed annoyance over the denial of the sacrament. It seemed an unnecessary imposition of a rule broken many times in the church. Dudley questioned continued attendance, but stopped his questions when he realized I was being blessed. After a time the pastor of the church did invite me to talk with him, and asked why I came. Then he began to give me names of people in his parish who needed prayer, a strange anomaly, since I could not receive the sacrament but could intercede for persons in need. Looking back on this experience, it seems a discipline which was necessary to fully appreciate the need for obedience in acts of devotion and in the willingness to be used apart from personal gain.

In the early search for the true meaning of prayer and health, Dudley and I faced the question of how to become involved in a movement that, so far as we could see, was frought with real hazards and questionable practices. We knew that many so-called faith healers had large movements and apparently exploited people in many ways. However, we also realized that the gospel and the Christian Church, particularly Methodism, contain a strong validation for this ministry. After a great deal of talk and consideration, Dudley finally concluded that I should have all the freedom and encouragement necessary to explore this movement, even if it involved some risk.

"But how will the church, especially its officials, react to the wife of one of its executives becoming involved in such undertakings?" I worried.

However, as my husband and I investigated some of the movements—for example, the Order of St. Luke of the Episcopal Church—we discovered a basic foundation solidly grounded in the life and liturgy of the church, supported by good scholarship and people who exhibited little of the sensationalism which we had thought characterized the healing ministry. To find knowledge, of course, we would have to become acquainted with groups on the fringe.

In addition, we found quite a wealth of literature, both in North America and Europe, on this subject. British sources were particularly helpful. Dudley and I also carefully read works by authors like Dr. Paul Tournier, the Swiss psychiatrist and lay theologian. So the search my husband and I began involved contacts with some risky movements, study of a variety of literature, and also direct encounter with whatever resources the churches of this country had to offer. This combination helped us to stabilize our own approach to and attitudes about spiritual healing. As our experience grew, we realized that the church had a great need for the healing ministry.

As the scarred areas of my body began to heal and the doctors could remove the dressings and bandages, I faced the possibility of again being able to dress—and to wear a brassiere. Dressing, which I had taken for granted before my operation, now posed a new challenge. The burns, high on my neck and back, left scars which my doctor said would remain for the rest of my life. Obviously I would have to take them into account in my dress.

First I had to learn to accept myself in the privacy of the bathroom, to see myself in the mirror and not look away; there in that intimate room I faced my greatest initial physical struggles. It took some time for me to acknowledge this reflection I saw in the mirror, and yet know in my spirit that it was in truth the temple of the Holy Spirit.

I shall always be grateful for the mother of one of Beverly's friends. She came and offered to take me to get properly fitted with a form and the brassiere which I now must wear. Her kindness softened this initial experience, my embarrassment and the startling bill. I realized that buying a brassiere was no longer a minor item in my wardrobe.

"Well, being a minster's wife should save you from the problem of discarding many of your dresses," my doctor kidded one day. "I presume you always wear a pretty high neck."

Laughing, I told him he was wrong. Through the years I wore and enjoyed wearing low-cut dresses. However, I decided to remove them from my closet so they wouldn't remind me of what I could no longer wear. I carefully selected people on whom I felt they would look nice and who would appreciate and enjoy them.

My disfigurement revealed a dimension of fear in people that I had not noticed before. How many women live in constant fear that this may happen to them! I discovered this in the dressing rooms of fine stores as sales clerks would gasp and suddenly leave as they saw the scars and burns. I soon learned to ask for the head sales person when I went into the department. I would explain to her that I had had a mastectomy and required certain types of clothes, and that I needed a mature saleslady whom my surgery would not upset. So I learned not only to protect them against shock, but also to protect myself against unpleasantness.

To ease my problem I picked up once again an art I had learned early in my youth, that of designing and making my own clothes. This released creative impulses and challenged me to design dresses with high style that did not accentuate the problem. I had to make sure that I was carrying the right weight on my left side so my body would be in balance and my shoulders held in right position.

Through the years, as I learned to prepare people by introduction and careful attention, I have had fewer unpleasant encounters. I have met with great understanding and retained my personal dignity. After unpleasant experiences in the early stages, shopping once again became an adventure and a joy.

However, buying a bathing suit presented a new problem. I searched to find an attractive one which would cover the scars from others' view and not expose my body to harmful rays of the sun. One of the most thrilling experiences during recovery came the day I put on my bathing suit and once again ran into the water. I felt sheer joy as I used my arms and felt my body move through the water. It was so much more than just physical exercise; it was an ecstasy that flowed through my whole being as though it moved with a life force propelled by delight.

The fact that I could no longer wear a low-cut dress for dinner or evening wear didn't stop me. I just reversed the dress, made a low-cut back, and found it just as attractive.

One of the most startling experiences came in my own

church circle. When I was able to attend the meetings again, I was surprised one day by a telephone call from the chairman, a woman I highly regarded for her leadership and honesty. She frankly told me that she wished I would join another group as she knew I was dying with cancer and the fact that I exhibited such joy and happiness deeply disturbed her. She could not reconcile the two. I waited until the change came about naturally. I learned also to contain myself when some well-wishing soul would come up close to me, peer into my eyes, and say, "Do you really feel as well as you look?" Or, "Your eyes are clear and your color is good." I resisted an impish urge to sometimes kick someone in the shins, or to show them the color of my tongue, because I had come to know the fear out of which they were motivated and the reassurance they sought for themselves.

I began to accept myself again, and realized in a new way the wonder of God's creation. I knew truly that people aren't just flesh and blood, but also spirit. By intermingling and balancing the physical body, mind, and spirit, one ultimately becomes a whole person in Christ.

During the first few months of my convalescence, someone sent me a magazine entitled *Sharing*. I had never seen it before or known about the healing work carried on for a number of years in the Episcopal Church. As I read about the work that Dr. Gaynor Banks and his wife had begun, it seemed something on which I could begin to gain some foundation in my search. Their work, which came out of deep theological research and study, was grounded in the church and in people, concerned as I was, about finding the truth. Thus, I wrote to Mrs. Banks.

I also read with great interest of the international conferences held in St. Stephen's Episcopal Church in Philadelphia over a number of years under the leadership of Dr. Alfred Price, Senior Warden of the Order of St. Luke. A prayer group, carried on in his church under disciplined order, accepted prayer requests, so I wrote and asked to be put on their prayer list.

One question at this time kept persisting in my mind, and I determinedly sought an answer in medical journals, books, and periodicals at local libraries. But nowhere did I find the answer to my question: What happens to the spiritual body of man when he is under an anesthetic? Does it make any difference that people are praying for you? Can you experience those prayers in the operating room? Can the physical, mental, and spiritual components of a person be anesthetized? Though I had now experienced six operations, I did not know for certain that prayer had made any difference in any one of them.

I recalled an experience in the hospital in Brooklyn when on a Monday morning a young lady appeared at my bed with a lovely bouquet of bronze mums from the altar of the Hanson Place Methodist Church. She came with the assurance that the congregation had offered special prayers for me on Sunday. I asked her about what time the people prayed, and she told me about 11:30. I recalled that at that time on this Sunday I *had* felt the power of prayer literally lifting my bed up to the throne of God. This feeling of the presence of power stayed with me all through the day and into the night.

"Did this really happen to me, or did I dream it?" I asked myself.

The bronze mums assured me that I had known the power of prayer at work. The church congregation had prayed, and I had received the confirmation of this prayer power in my hospital room.

Now, however, I wanted to know prayer power in its relevancy to the operating room. During these months a growth appeared on my left elbow. It did not give me any physical pain, but I soon became concerned about it. I noticed the eyes and faces of my family and others as they saw something abnormal again growing on my body. I went to see my doctor, who urged its removal. I recall a great calm about this, and my shock at the reactions of some people. One lady visited me in great distress, believing that surely now I was going to lose my arm with cancer. She told me of a lady she knew who had had this experience and was still enjoying life and looking nice even though she now had only one arm. Other people began to feel sorry for me, expressing their consternation at how far God was going to punish or deal with me. Was there some deep sin I did not even know of myself? People seemed to think God was spitting out all his wrath on me, and they could not understand it, for in their eyes I was a good person.

Dudley got caught up in this same frantic anxiety for a few days, too, and thought I must have this taken care of immediately. But I decided to wait, so the doctor scheduled this operation for September 9, my birthday. I knew this operation would not be anything really dangerous, or involve any suffering. I believed this operation would be performed so that I would forever have the answer to my question.

"I will give you the answer," the Lord told me. "In this operation they will perform you will know the answer to your question."

I went into the surgery feeling that it was a wonderful opportunity, a real adventure with my Lord, to find out whether or not prayer and prayer power are effective under anesthesia. On the morning of the operation the nurses came with the injections and drugs; for the first time in my experience they also blindfolded me. Even at that time I felt a consciousness that transcended anything physical, from the very beginning a new experience for me. As attendants wheeled me into the operating room and administered pentothal, I was conscious and fully aware of the work going on. I transcended the physical body, as though my spirit body was lifted above, fully conscious and witnessing the entire operation. Back in the recovery room, I remember calling a nurse to my side and asking her to go see my husband and tell him exactly what happened during the operation, that he should not be concerned, that everything was just fine. She patted me on the arm, then disappeared.

Finally, when I went back into my room, I asked Dudley, "Did they come to tell you or give you my message?"

"No, no one has told me anything," he replied.

"Oh, I'll tell you all about it," I said. "It went off just great."

While I talked about the operation, the phone rang. Dudley answered and was astounded when the doctor reiterated what I had told him in detail. Later on a lady doctor stood at the side of my bed.

"Mrs. Ward, you don't know me, but I am on Dr. Rosi's staff."

"Oh yes, I do know you."

"No, you've never met me before."

"I do know you! You were in the operating room and I know exactly what you did in the operation. You prepared my arm for surgery, and then when the lump was removed, you sewed up the incision."

"Why, how could you know that? You were blindfolded and under anesthetic!"

"I know because I saw the entire operation."

"You couldn't have possibly seen!"

"Will you tell me one thing. Were you aware of a power, a presence in the operating room while I was there?"

"Yes, it was so manifest that each one of us commented on it."

Later I shared this conversation with the surgeon and we talked further. A man of prayer, he confirmed that many times in his work he has asked the same question of God and of himself. He had no verification of it any more than I had had in my search, but my knowing, my experience, meant a great deal to him.

The day I had the surgery was the opening of the interna-

72

tional conference in Philadelphia, and I had requested special prayers for that day. I had received assurance of this from both Dr. Price and Mrs. Banks. Dudley lectured at DePauw in the Indiana Pastors' School on the days before the surgery, and a number of the ministers met for prayer early on the morning of surgery. Through this operation I had received an answer to my question.

Sometimes later I received my first call to visit a person who had cancer, the caretaker in the church where we belonged. Since the request posed a real challenge and something of a threat, I didn't say immediately that I would go. I prayed for several days before I arrived at a place where I felt free to go without communicating fear to him. Fortunately, when I went for the first time, he was alone, and we established a relationship at that time which would become enriched in the months ahead. I asked him if I could get something for him.

"There is one thing, Mrs. Ward, that I've never owned, a Bible. Would you get me a Bible? I don't know whether anyone in the church really loves me, even though I've worked there for seventeen years. I don't want them to know that I never had a Bible, so please don't tell anybody, or don't tell anyone of my fear about love."

I went home, got a Phillips translation of the New Testament which I had recently purchased, and took it to him with a card with the twenty-third psalm on it. We read the psalm together, and I told him about my experience with the Good Shepherd and what He had meant to me. I left him with the instruction that each time before he read the Bible, he should first read the twenty-third psalm. I assured him, as one member of the congregation, that I loved him and I knew that if I loved him, other people loved him too. He must begin to believe this, I said, and people would respond to his belief.

In the next few weeks wonderful things happened. The high school boys took over his work as janitor so he was not threatened with the loss of his job; after he went home, people drove him back and forth to the hospital for his treatment; other people took over the arrangement for the suitable food and running errands for him. His wife had been ill for years, but few in the church knew about it. Now they began to show kindness to her. Lawyers offered to come to help straighten out his financial affairs. Other persons began a fund so that in case of his death, his widow would be secure. People began to relate, not to his disease, but to the man, George Heisler, in a loving and creative way that thrilled his soul and did amazing things for everyone involved. During my last visit to George, his wife said in a simple way, "Why did this happen to my George? He has always been good, and he has never done anything bad. Why would God do this to him?"

"I don't know the answer to your question," I replied, "but I do know that a year ago George was not prepared to meet his God as he is today. Cancer has eaten away at his physical body, has caused pain and suffering, but through it George has seen the power of love that does exist in the hearts of men. As this love was expressed on the human level, George was better able to comprehend the great love of Jesus. He came to know and to accept Christ as his personal friend and Savior."

While the cancer destroyed his physical body, his spirit body was set free for a tremendous witness to people, a witness that will never die. George, in the months that he lived, read all the New Testament and developed a wonderful light in his face. One day, with a voice strong with conviction, he said to me, "Mrs. Ward, I have read not only all the New Testament that you gave me, but I know it because you told me about the Good Shepherd. I know the Bible and I know him."

George's last spoken words were to my husband: "Pastor, what can we do for all these other men in the room who have my disease, but not my hope?" George died a healed, whole person.

Another group with which I came in contact through a member of our prayer group was the Spiritual Frontiers Fellowship. The knowledge that such a group existed, with high principles and reputable and responsible people in charge, encouraged me. I learned that I and others in the group shared similar gifts, which I had received in childhood or at birth. At times these had puzzled and frightened me and I had never fully understood what they involved. I remember the consternation, even as a small child, in realizing that maybe I was different from other people. Other people didn't see things that I saw, or hear the things I heard. Through the years I had hidden many of these things, trying to conceal these spiritual gifts, but now I began to see them as something special.

In September, 1961, we moved from Wilmette, Illinois, to Washington, D.C., after the merger of the Boards of Temperance, Peace, and Social and Economic Relations into one Board of Christian Social Concerns. I not only found it hard to leave my Chicago doctors, in whom I had such confidence, but also the different groups to which I had related and from whom I received spiritual strength and inspiration. The move, though, brought other possibilities. Almost immediately I realized that I could attend the International Conference at St. Stephen's Church in Philadelphia that year. How thrilling to meet many of the people about whom I had read, and to hear them speak!

6 | NEW DISCOVERIES IN THE NATION'S CAPITAL

In the capital city setting Dudley soon experienced a new dimension in his work and a new challenge to his faith. One Friday afternoon, while in his office in the Methodist Building between the Supreme Court and the new Senate Office Building on Capitol Hill, Dudley received a call from New York. A National Council of Churches representative asked whether he could come that evening to a meeting at which Negro civil rights leaders would present an appeal to religious leaders much like the one they had made to Attorney General Robert Kennedy shortly before.

Responding to the call, Dudley left for the airport, caught a plane, and arrived at eight o'clock in Harlem, where he entered a room with about twenty-five other people, many of them aggressive, diligent, dedicated black civil rights workers. All that evening he heard the devastating story of repudiation by these black leaders of the church and the white leadership of our nation. Dudley felt shocked by the encounter, as the conviction that consumed these black leaders got through as never before to the white churchmen. During the meeting demonstrations by extremist groups occurred on several street corners near the meeting place.

"When I left that place, I realized that I had had an experience such as I had never known before," Dudley told me later. "I knew that I would probably never be the same again."

After the meeting Dudley took the first plane back to Washington, arriving shortly after daybreak. He had slept only a short while. During the whole day he seemed in a kind of stupor, still feeling the effects of the late night meeting.

"Something has happened to you," I said, noticing his appearance, and he replied that it certainly had.

That evening Dudley took a plane to Louisville, Kentucky, to participate in services the following day in one of our churches and to receive an "Ambassador of Goodwill" award from the mayor of the city.

"As I traveled in the plane, I was completely removed from all events going on around me," Dudley told me. "I could sense that some significant spiritual breakthrough was about to occur, but I didn't know what form it would take.

"I checked in at the Sheraton-Jefferson Hotel in Louisville, went to my room, and spent the next two and one half hours on the phone with leaders of the struggle in Mississippi, some of whom were facing arrest while others were already in jail. At 11:30 P.M. I went to bed and fell into a deep sleep.

"About 1:30 A.M. I awoke with a sense of a great Presence in the room, which I recognized as the Spirit of God. It was so real that I got out of bed completely refreshed, sat in a chair, and felt a stream of spiritual power which I had never experienced before. The whole room came alive with this reality. Then I knew a completely different dimension of spiritual reality from anything I had ever experienced before. I also knew that my work could never again be the same because I realized that I must include an active, thoroughgoing relationship with the Holy Spirit."

Dudley was tempted to call me immediately in Washington to tell me about this thrilling experience, but he waited until 7:00 A.M. When he called, I knew he expected to tell me what happened, but I answered the phone with these words: "Did He come?"

"Yes," Dudley replied, startled that I would have an idea of what occurred.

"He came here, too."

I explained that I had also awakened with the realization of the Presence and had gotten out of bed to sit on the floor, which I often do in my devotional periods. I, too, felt the vitality of the Spirit in our bedroom and knew that a new direction had come in our search. Dudley and I checked our time and realized that the event had occurred in Washington and Louisville at precisely the same time. We had waited for this great day, and it had come the first Saturday of June, 1963.

Thinking about this experience later, Dudley and I realized that it, combined with other events which took place in following months—including the opportunity to become involved in Foundry Methodist Church in a healing ministry with the full cooperation of the Rev. Edward W. Bauman—was another turning point in our lives and work.[1]

In the wonder and mystery of the Spirit we became part of a fellowship and began to share in the fullness of Christ. We soon clearly understood that the Spirit is not bound by man-made rules, but moves with transcendant power through and beyond them to achieve his purpose and make his power known. The one thing required of us was to be faithful and obedient to our Lord. As opportunities came to pray for others,

---

[1] In the Appendix, an article which appeared in the magazine *Church and Home*, September, 1968, provides a description of this work.

78

Dudley and I wished that I had the physical strength to visit them as I had done in the years of our pastoral ministry. But He made it known to us that at no time had we, through our physical presence, brought healing to any man. He was not diminishing any of the former work, but was rather revealing to us, and especially to me, a great truth. God and God alone, working through an individual, transforms a condition or situation. He is not limited by time or space.

During the following months I learned the ministry of prayer for those in need; I did this in the privacy and silence of my room, first during stated times of prayer. Later, as I received requests at all hours of the day, I began slowly to learn the meaning, power, and command of our Lord to pray without ceasing. I have seen that God can and does use effectively the healed consciousness of the person who offers himself in the silence for others. However, to continue to grow and reach out with the good news, a person must share in the wider fellowship of the concerned. I felt an urgent desire within me to be part of the prayer fellowship for others.

I first thought of those with whom I would like to pray, both in and out of the church. To those with whom I spoke, I talked about this type of fellowship. They usually responded that if they could catch their breath in all the round of activities, they would happily join, but they couldn't possibly take on anything more in their already jammed schedules.

One morning I sat feeling discouraged at the kitchen table and told the Lord about the futility of my search. Suddenly the telephone rang and a lady asked if she might stop by the house. As we sat talking about the need in her life, I realized that I should speak to her about a prayer group. She responded with joy, and we agreed to meet the next Wednesday morning for an hour. One of the women she had previously approached, on hearing of the meeting, asked to be included.

As the three of us gathered the first morning, someone knocked at the door. Answering it, I greeted a neighbor holding a letter she had just received and needing some help. I invited her in, and she became the fourth member of the group. The Spirit led each participant, and He has done this in the years that followed as several groups developed, averaging about seven in each and meeting weekly. Each group has kept a strict discipline of time, schedule, and prayer. Each member has come out of a different background, vocation, church, but all have held certain common central desires—to learn more about prayer, to pray effectively for others, and to become a channel for this power to others. As they met, the Spirit began to move in their midst; they felt his power in their homes and families, and ultimately reached out into the lives of those for whom they prayed.

At historic St. John's Episcopal Church in Lafayette Square, across from the White House, the Order of St. Luke met once a month on Sunday afternoon. One evening Dr. Alfred Price, the Senior Warden of the Order, came from Philadelphia to speak and conduct a healing service. That night I became a member of the Order of St. Luke and was inducted into the order by Dr. Price.

Through Dr. Albert Day I learned of the Fellowship of the Healing Christ and later received an invitation from this group to come to Chattanooga to speak at an induction service in Centenary Methodist Church. There I met a young woman named Oma Belle, who had cancer of the face. Her minister of twenty-two years invited me to accompany him to visit her. As we drove across the city, he told of all that he had done and indicated that he and the doctors could do no more. He was taking me to see her at the request of the family, and he shared with me many of their doubts and their fears.

A letter which he wrote several months after Oma Belle's death, explained his reaction to my visit:

I shall never forget that meeting; when you entered the room, I saw plenty, although I was unable to see all that took place. Her face shone with new hope; there was no need to establish rapport, because it appeared as though you had known one another for many years. I stood in amazement as I looked and listened; I knew something was taking place beyond human knowledge. Although this encounter did not bring outward physical healing, and her last days were filled with suffering, I feel that she found the secret of life that day and was never alone again.

Oma Belle had anticipated my coming. As I walked into the room with her pastor, it suddenly seemed filled with a presence other than ourselves. As I took her hand in mine, she looked up into my eyes and said, "You know, don't you?" I answered, "Yes," and she said, "All these months I knew that one day someone would come to stand beside my bed and take my hand so that I would never again be alone."

This experience transformed me. I found I did not relate to her out of sympathy or out of the fact that I, too, had known cancer. Rather, the power of the Presence so vibrant in the room moved through the Christ within me and witnessed to the Christ within her. In this moment of time, it seemed we had known one another for eternities. This oneness we experienced that day transcended time and space. Later I awoke many times in the night realizing that Oma Belle needed prayer. Although I was in Washington and she in Chattanooga, Tennessee, my prayer spanned the distance. Often she would say to her pastor the next morning, "It wasn't so bad last night because Alice Ward came and stood beside my bed, held my hand, and prayed for me."

After reading Katherine Kuhlman's book, *I Believe in Miracles,* I wanted to meet this lady, so I visited Pittsburgh and attended her healing service. Although this service was different from our regular church service, one could not deny the presence of the power of God and its manifestations in the hearts, the minds, and the physical bodies of many of the people present.

Before I met her, I felt a spiritual kinship to this woman, who had a commanding authority about her that was communicated in her speech and manner, and in her dealings with people in their difficulties. Others throughout the entire auditorium picked this up, not in an emotional way, but in such a manner that you felt the Spirit of God present and moving in the lives of people. Later in visiting with her in her home, I felt I was with one of the great spirits of our time.

In nearby Baltimore I found one of my richest contacts and friendships in the healing ministry at the home of Ambrose and Olga Worrall. Harper and Row in 1966 published the story of their lives and healing work—*The Gift of Healing*. We discovered in one another a kindred spirit and a concern for people, the church, and especially our own Methodist Church. Through the years they have sustained me in prayer and have often shared with me in prayer requests that I felt I could not meet myself. At no time, day or night, have they refused to share, always in joy and with a spontaneous response to any request I might make of them.

The spirit in which these two people have shared their lives and work inspired me. So often in the healing ministry only one of a marriage partnership shows a continued interest. Yet Ambrose and Olga Worrall beautifully complemented each other. As a result their prayer time at nine o'clock each evening is filled with great unity in silence and spiritual power. I, too, longed for the time when Dudley would feel that we could complement each other in this ministry.

As my physical strength returned, opportunities came for me to speak to different groups. One, offered by the Rev. Claus Rohlfs, was the Healing Conference at the Methodist Retreat Center in Kerrville, Texas. I also became a pupil during this period, since Dr. Klaus Thomas from Berlin, one of the chaplains of the Order of St. Luke, was in America teaching at Wesley Seminary in Washington, and I took the courses He offered. As my work and interest became known in this field, the demand for teaching, counseling, and prayer increased. Though this work offered many rewards and compensations, especially spiritual ones, it also had many hazards, not the least of them the temptation to accept material gifts. I remained firm in my conviction that God gave this gift I had; it was not mine, and I must not receive anything of material nature for it. I effectively used my gift on the spiritual level. This power was conducted *through* me; I had no power in myself, so I could not accept anything from anyone in compensation for something that in essence was not mine.

This attitude became a problem to many people as they could not understand why they should not pay for my prayer. Obviously theirs was not an expression of thanks to God for his goodness, but rather a result of a desire to buy my services or purchase the assurance that I would faithfully pray for them. I always carefully informed people that, having no power of my own, I prayed in the name and through the power of Jesus Christ. Through prayer I would bring them into the presence of the Christ. Alice Ward as an individual would be completely out of the picture. They would be relating in the prayer request to Christ himself—not to me.

This frightened some people. They said they didn't mind coming into relationship with me (whom they saw as some kind of good person) and believed my prayers surely would help them through their difficulty, disorder, or inconvenience, but they did not wish to become involved with a power they could not see, touch, or control. Often when I explained to them how I prayed and in what power I prayed, they would, like Nicodemus, steal off into the night.

To establish contact with doctors in the Washington area,

I was referred to cancer specialists at Johns Hopkins University. Every three months I went for an examination. I clearly explained to them, as I had to my previous doctors, that I put neither my life nor my fate in their hands, that I had a higher loyalty in my life—the Christ within me. My body was the temple of his Spirit. I wanted them to relate to me in the same spirit.

Over the years I observed many people as they have come and gone in cancer clinics. Waiting for the service of these eminent specialists in their beautiful suites of offices, I have felt troubled many times about the attitudes we have here in America regarding preventive medicine and the fear often transferred to people by doctors themselves.

"Well, I can live for another three months and enjoy myself."

"He said everything is all right."

Then a woman who went in composed comes out, and her appearance indicates that she received disturbing news. She's nervous, and the fears show as she speaks to the nurse and tries to remember dates or perhaps even her phone number. The fear is picked up by the people with her, and patients in the waiting room become conscious of the woman's disturbance.

On many occasions I have spoken to the doctors directly about this situation, and in most cases I've received this answer: "Mrs. Ward, we have too many people coming to and going from our offices to do the personal work that you think should be done before they leave this office. The only way we can be sure of getting them back here is to scare them to death."

Thus, I came to realize that all the worldly knowledge and learning does not in itself dissipate or transmute the fears within a man's conscious and subconscious mind. Often the most learned doctor in cancer research has this fear within him and can unconsciously transfer it to other people.

I became aware of this great fear within the subconscious mind of one of my doctors, and even felt it being transferred to me through his hands when he would touch my body. This new revelation confronted me with a problem; I had to make certain decisions. Although this doctor's competence in this field of knowledge was beyond reproach, I knew that any further contact might possibly germinate the potential fear within me, feed into disease and disharmony, and increase my weakness. I spent hours one day walking around Johns Hopkins Hospital. I did not find my answer easily. Finally, I went into the little church across the street from the hospital and knelt at the altar, where I reached certain decisions.

First of all, I decided I would not let this particular doctor touch my physical body again. I would also make no decision regarding X-ray or further examination out of fear. Somehow I must become a whole person again. The division within my physical body was also being transferred to other aspects of my life.

The fact that I could no longer relate to one single doctor as a whole person fragmented other parts of my being. I felt I must come to a doctor for treatment as a whole person in order to experience a dimension of healing that had to begin at the very center of my life. I had read much about this disease and what scientific research had discovered. The study of the cells of the body interested me and I began to ask: If cancer basically is immature baby cells that have gone wild, what about the other cells of the body? Frankly, I found very little written or discussed about the mature, healthy cells of the body, especially in cancer research. I searched in various places for information, but felt I could learn most through the Creator himself.

As I grew in prayer and came to know the power of silence, and how to be still and know that the Lord is, I arrived at the place where I could sit silently in the direct presence of God, and listen to him as he revealed great truths to me about the cells. Edison once declared that "every cell thinks." I began to understand that every cell is a universe within itself, separate and individual, with a marvelous intelligence working instinctively for the health and wholeness of my being. Certain cells have special functions, but they all operate by instinctive intelligence.

I realized that if this is true, one could also speak to one's cells and that the cells depended very much on what a person thought and also the words he used in the patterns of his thought processes. Gradually I began to know how to relate to this truth and how to deal with the thought patterns, actions, and ways of reaction. No immediate great change took place, but as my study and application progressed, I realized that change was coming from within. Several of the ways in which I had thought and reacted conflicted with the laws of health and power. Many of the thought patterns, negative reactions, and concepts were in themselves diminishing to the building of healthy new cells. I was in a measure responsible for their weakness because I had related to many things of a destructive nature after thinking I was doing good or helping someone.

I began to know in my deeds for others, and even in my prayer life, that I was being identified not to health, light, and love but rather to that which was diseased, disharmonious and destructive. Slowly I began to comprehend that I must enter a level of consciousness through the Spirit of God within me and the grace of God working through me. Only then could I concentrate and commune with God. Only then could the Spirit of God use me to increase the healing light, power, and love within another person without identifying myself physically and spiritually with the disease and disharmony operating within that other person.

I received one other revelation. I came from a family lineage and heritage of deep and profound spiritual background, a fact of which I became fully aware when I began to relate myself to this new phase of consciousness. The Spirit of God revealed to me the spiritual heritage from which I had come and showed me the gifts that had been entrusted to this line of people, many of them passed on to me.

This revelation carried with it a great responsibility—these cells, the light cells within the body, were also the heritage I would pass on to my family. They are my real spiritual wealth and heritage, and only as I keep them, care for them, and allow them to grow can I pass them on through the spirit to those who come after me. In no way are these mine to use or to boast about; they are a gift of God entrusted to me in my time on this earth. Only as I am completely attune with God and as I commune with him and live in relationship to him can these cells and these gifts I have received come into their full radiance and beauty. My power increases in the spirit as the cells of the body are transmuted into light cells and energized by the Spirit of the Living God.

These limited insights in no way set aside the laws of nature or the processes of the physical body and the care of it. I diligently and systematically followed instructions from my medical doctors.

In this period of time, after six years with no physical signs of cancer's return, my insurance policy, taken out many years ago, became paid up. I decided that I had always had insurance and saw no reason why I should not have insurance again, although different people in my family and outside thought that it was rather ridiculous for me to try to get another life insurance policy. I decided to try and set out to apply for a new policy. Only one insurance agent, who was especially energetic, felt I could get one, perhaps from a New York group or from an unheard-of company. However, I maintained that unless I could get insurance from one of the best companies, I didn't wish to have it. I went through all the tests and examinations required, and within a short time I was given a two-thousand-dollar life insurance policy, a great event in my life. For me this was a definite sign of healing.

This seemed to disturb some of my doctors, and from then on they asked me to get X-rays of the chest and breast every three months. This intensifying of my checkups I felt was basically unnecessary. Out of this demand I began to question the relationship to different doctors for separate organs of my body. They did not know one another, never came together to discuss their findings of the separate parts of my body, and never, it seemed, put all my parts back together again or looked at me as a person. I became fragmented, and in my mind I saw myself here and there, like Humpty-Dumpty, never put together again. I instinctively felt opposed to concentration of so much attention on the right breast. If the cancer spread, it would not necessarily attack there first. I knew within myself, though the doctors maintained that I had no way of determining this, that the spread of cancer would not come there. To concentrate on this one part of my body seemed almost suicide to me.

I had faced the question of a hysterectomy at the time of the radical mastectomy on my left breast. At that time a couple of young interns had come into my room one morning and suggested that I immediately have such an operation. I had asked them whether or not their wives had all their reproductive organs and, rather gleefully, they both said, "Oh yes, we're expecting to raise a family."

"When John was born six years ago," I retorted, my reproductive organs were healthy, and I have no reason to believe today that they are unhealthy. Unless the doctors can prove to me that there is sound reason for removing them, I think I shall keep them."

Holding to this decision, I could not immediately quiet all the fears that had been created. By keeping my own counsel, not seeking other advice, I gradually mastered the fear and

88

gained assurance that such fear-motivated surgery would at present achieve little.

I knew within myself I would face still another crisis. It seemed I could not escape this. I also knew that I had a choice on how to relate to what lay ahead. I determined to handle it differently than before. The resources and strength, and also the weaknesses that I had discerned both within and without myself, would help me face the approaching crisis.

7 | THE CLOUD GATHERS WITH LIGHT IN IT

The first inner awareness of what was confronting me in the months ahead came in November, 1964, when I decided that this three-month pattern of X-raying the right breast had to stop. I did not do this as an act of rebellion, but rather as a decision regarding my physical body in relationship to this disease. Although for many months I carried in my purse the medical slips which would have obtained these X-rays for me free at the hospital, I fought the battle over again as to whether or not I should just go and have them done.

I had to confront and answer more than just a physical question. It would have been relatively easy to have gone, had the X-rays, and said, "Well, that's that—there's nothing to worry about." But that would have been an escape, proving nothing. I felt I had to feel something more basic and fundamental in this whole thing; I could not use the X-rays as an escape.

I had no indication of any physical trouble until one day when I had gone to Baltimore to attend a luncheon on Washington's Birthday. Dudley was on his way to a National Council meeting in Portland, Oregon, and John had asked to go to the home of his scout leader to spend part of the day with his friend, the scoutmaster's son. The teen-age brother of John's friend had made a homemade rocket, which the boys, thinking it would be a wonderful way to celebrate the holiday, took to the school yard and set off. The rocket did not go off as planned, and a piece of lead pipe struck John in the head, penetrating the skull, causing a serious injury.

One of the lasting impressions that John has of this accident is summed up in the question, "Why didn't somebody help me?" He was conspicuously wounded and lost one quart of blood. He, with his friend, walked two blocks down a busy street and no person volunteered to assist him. And he didn't ask.

At precisely the same time this accident happened, I was sitting at the table in the church. The minister on my right asked me to tell about a healing that had happened a few years before to a boy who had had brain trouble and was facing surgery. I could not speak at that moment and just sat dumb with a pain coming into my head that I knew did not belong to me. It came with increased heat and intensity, making it impossible for me to speak, and for a few moments I just stared at the people.

Mentally, I began to release this pain, telling the Lord it was not mine, that I gave it to him, asking him to take care of this pain on my right forehead. As I looked up after explaining to the others that the story was too long to tell at that time, a lady stood before me.

"Are you Mrs. Ward?" I nodded in the affirmative and she said, "You are wanted on the telephone."

The telephone hung in the kitchen where the ladies busily handled pots and pans. All I could tell from the phone call was that John was hurt and in the hospital. Taken to a nearby, quiet home, I talked to our doctor in Washington. He confirmed the seriousness of the injury and also accepted my permission to

91

procure the best neurosurgeon in Washington. I left immediately by taxi for Washington.

Fortunately, our doctor and minister were at the hospital, so John was surrounded by people whom he knew and whom he knew loved him. I arrived in record time, and when I came into the room, John smiled at me.

"Mother, take both of your hands and put them, one on each side of my head." John knows the healing power which is transmitted through the spiritual energies of God in me.[1]

I did this for a little while.

"Now, that's enough, just take them away."

John had me do this several times before he went into surgery at five o'clock. Just before he went into surgery, he

---

[1] The following is Dudley's account of his experience with this power. This incident happened at the dedication of the Church Center for the United Nations building in New York.

"I had worked very late and long hours to get all the details in readiness for the service on Sunday at which the Secretary of State would be present, the Secretary General of the United Nations, the Governor of New York, the U. S. delegate to the United Nations, the Hon. Adlai Stevenson, and many of the top church dignitaries from various denominations and churches. Over two thousand people were expected, and more than that attended. I not only worked long hours, but was carrying the load of all the details and the time element was vital. I awakened in the morning with a slight fever, but had to be up early and was out making the necessary preparations. When I came back about noon, I had developed chills and the fever had increased. I, of course, was anxious, and I doubted whether or not I could go on with the affair. Alice asked me to lie down upon the bed and when she quieted me and talked with me about the necessary relaxation and faith in God, she laid her hands upon me and prayed. A vital current of energy coursed through my being. I fell into a very deep sleep which lasted about forty-five minutes. Alice sat in the room and kept a silent, prayerful vigil during all that time. When I awakened, I was completely free of the fever, and all anxiety and fear. My entire body was filled with energy. I dressed, and was able to attend the ceremonies and handle all the details to my own and others' complete satisfaction."

asked me a question I shall never forget: "Mother, is anyone praying for me?"

The people of our church were wonderful; an eminent doctor came and sat in the room with me during the four hours of surgery. Since Dudley could not get plane reservations to bring him to Washington that night, and did not arrive until the next morning, Dr. Grover Bagby, one of my husband's colleagues, came and stayed with me and John through the long hours of the night. John came through the surgery well. The doctor removed any fragmented bone and reported good chances for full recovery. As I recall that night, I remember the wonderful spirit of Dr. Bagby, the calm and peace which permeated the room.

I also remember that night as one of laying-on of hands. John seemed to know instinctively where I should put my hands, how long I should leave them, and continually he would call for me to place my hands on different parts of his body and to leave them there just so long. Then he would say, "That's enough, Mother, take them off now." On this night of victory I watched my boy move through those hours and respond to my questions and also to the nurses and doctors. I felt, with the coming of dawn, his healing was within him. Good care, common sense, and the divine intelligence within this boy would assure recovery.

Following this experience and in the weeks of John's convalescence, I began to sense a numbness in my right thumb and forefinger that had not been there before. I knew it had a relationship to something within my head structure. This became apparent in the different things I did, such as sewing and pinning up my hair, since I had to buy larger pins so that I could grip them. I told no one because I knew this was not the time to enter into any medical situation. I realized also that the evidence of the cancer in other parts of my body than the breast vindicated my conviction that my whole body needed to be treated as a unit.

Dianne had just announced her engagement; her wedding date was set for August. I wanted to function as a mother dreams of doing through this period of her daughter's life. However, in my prayer life I began to ask God to direct me to the attention and into the confidence of a doctor—one who would accept me as a whole person, not one who was a cancer specialist of one particular organ of the body. At times it seemed I was asking for an impossibility, but I persisted in my prayer and received the answer.

The first indication to my family of my new difficulty came one Saturday night in May when a terrible pain convulsed me as I got up from the table to get my husband a cup of coffee. This pain lasted for some time and was so severe that Dudley ran and grabbed the phone.

"No, don't do that, you must not call the doctor!"

I knew that once a doctor related to the situation, I would lose all choice and control. The pain passed; although it weakened me, we went on with our normal way of life and did not discuss it further. On several occasions in June the same pain returned with similar intensity. Again we called no doctor. Dudley and I both knew the power of prayer together, and I had asked people, disciplined in prayer, to pray. I was enabled to transmute[2] the pain and, when it passed, to be re-energized, allowing me to carry on my daily and my family living in a normal, natural way.

---

[2] "Transmute" has a special meaning. It refers back to the work of the ancient alchemists who tried to change base metal into gold. As it has been incorporated into the vocabulary of prayer and health, it means literally that physically, spiritually, emotionally, and socially, the dross of life can be eliminated, and a precious new element of energy and health becomes part of human experience as God's vital Spirit is received and given freedom in a life.

94

The weekend of July 4 became a time of contrast and decision making that set the course for the next several weeks. Dudley was scheduled to go on a speaking engagement that would necessitate being away most of that week. I hoped that the difficulty would remain quiet during this period. However, it flared up so severely that Dudley canceled the initial first days of his conference and insisted that I see a doctor. I went to our family doctor for the first time, and he suggested abdominal X-rays. We went to the nearby hospital, and, to satisfy my husband further, I also had the chest X-rays taken that I had skipped in the previous months. Fortunately, one of our doctor friends was at the hospital and read the X-rays for us. We were amazed to find, in spite of all the distress I had experienced, clear X-rays, showing only a few pockets of gas in the abdominal area. He said a very mild medication could remedy this. I felt I had been given time. Dudley left that night more relaxed for his meetings. I took the initiative and at that time resolved the course my life would take over the next few weeks.

I first prepared to take a trip to visit my family in Canada and then devote myself to the wedding. My nearing crisis was ever present, because the sudden stabs of pain came more frequently in the night than during daytime. I felt two types of pain in this ordeal. I suffered the physical pain, and literally rolled with agony on the floor, but my husband had to go through the experience of seeing this happen while bound by my decision not to call a doctor.

We knew that if a doctor came into the situation, he would have to act on his ethic to relive the pain. This would lift me out of the family and the wedding preparations, which I did not wish to happen. We learned that pain, for the one going through it and for the one who has to sit and watch the other person suffer, can be transmuted; with the change comes a great quietness and calm. My energy and vitality were amazingly restored. I would find in the mornings a new spirit of relaxation as I again entered the day's work.

During all this time we received revealing guidance from the Holy Spirit, even on Dianne's wedding gown. I saw the gown in my mind's eye and knew which store it was in. One day I said, "Dianne, we'll go today and get your wedding gown." Although she tried on several gowns as attendants brought them in, I still knew that the right one had not come. Then the clerk brought in another gown; Dianne put it over her head and saw it was perfect in every detail, requiring not one change or alteration. It was just as I had seen it. There have been many times when guidance has come on more important matters. But this one illustrated so fully that God's care is related to every experience of our lives.

The same thing occurred with all the shopping. Many days I would feel well in the morning, and following the guidance to go to a certain store, we would find the things we needed. Just relating in obedience became a great adventure. The guidance meant no waste of energy, unnecessary frustration, or sense of futility. In the midst of these days we found the adventuresome companionship of the Spirit. I knew literally that I was not walking alone, the Lord was with me, so much a part of everything I did. It was never a case of trying to prove my strength or denying one situation to escape into another; it was instead a transcendent experience.

I could not escape, of course, the reality of suffering. The day would come when I would face it, but now there was this event of joy, happiness, beauty, vitality, and love in the emergence of a new home, and this prospect was an inspiration itself. Involved in another person's joy and dreams, I held a transcendent power that somehow picked me up and carried me on. I have often thought that any event, no matter how much it might pull a person down or lessen him or her, stands opposite another event set over and above, which has transcendent elements in it. We can always choose the one to which we relate.

This conviction has been part of my life for many years. On one of my trips to Canada about ten years ago, I had seen a little brass cross in a craft shop, and knew I would buy it. This cross just fitted into the palm of my hand, yet it had weight and substance, no markings, no form, but the simplicity of straight lines. I have carried this cross with me. Often in prayer, in church, or traveling, I would rest it in my hand. In nights of pain, of diagnosis or surgery, that cross was with me, although only I knew of its presence. Not that I attributed to the piece of metal in itself any power, but I found that many times in listening to the analysis of the doctor or as he spoke about the disease which I confronted, I would reach into my purse and take the cross in my hand. This always seemed to help me focus my attention and emotions on the news the doctor gave me. As I put my hand on the cross, the message came to me. I did not have to strain to think about the elements in the cross, but about the reality of my physical condition. My hope lay not ultimately in any medical or scientific answer, although I did not deny any available help; but I refused to pin all my hopes on any one thing. The Cross was central to my life; it was in my hand and held the ultimate victory of my life and of my death.

Throughout my crises I carefully considered and appreciated the advances made in science, the prescribed medication or therapy that I could use in the attempt to heal my physical body. I had learned, however, in a real sense to relate myself daily to a transcendent event, and for me the event became the Cross, because I knew it holds the ultimate victory for every man, even the whole world.

In these weeks the family found themselves working with one another in a lively relationship. Each one assumed responsibility, and a real maturing took place in us all. The fact that I did not seek any special attention gave me a freedom to move in and out of the events and to go places and do things without questions or restrictions. In not asking anyone for sympathy or special consideration, I had a refreshing freedom and strength in movement.

However, as the wedding day drew near, anyone who saw me could tell that I had liver trouble. The one prayer request I made, and for which I prayed definitely, was that on the wedding day my eyes and my skin might be clear and that I would receive vitality and joy for the day.

The wedding day was beautiful, guests arrived, and we began to dress and prepare for the ceremony, remembering the rehearsal and party of the previous night. Everything seemed perfect—excitement, joy for another person, and the pride of the family together. I remember an awareness of the flood of energy that came to me, something not of myself. When I dressed I saw my clear skin and knew that God had answered my prayers. How thankful I felt that God had heard even that little request. More than our daughter's lovely marriage and the nice wedding for people to see and enjoy, it represented to us as a family many victories achieved together in the transcendent power to which we had related.

While our daughter and her husband honeymooned, we traveled to Virginia Beach for a few days so John and Dudley could enjoy some fishing and Beverly and her friend could enjoy swimming and the sun. Although I enjoyed walks along the beach, I had to take most meals in the hotel room because the pains now came more severely and at closer intervals. I knew the crisis was nearing, but I continued praying that I would be able to relate to one doctor as a whole person. I knew that whatever I faced, I could only meet it with a sense of victory as I confronted it in this way. Our family doctor consented to my entrance into the hospital under his name. I felt that this was the answer to prayer I had so long sought;

a strange happiness and strength I had not known before filled my body.

The spread of disease, not just internal, had become noticeable. My skin had become a deep yellow and extremely sensitive. At times it seemed that a liquid fire would literally pass through my body, and my skin would become so sensitive that a touch or scratch would cause it to become raw and bleed. I had known for some weeks that this involved the skull structure of my head as well as the liver. This became noticeable when a blood vessel burst and spread throughout my eyes, causing discoloration and swelling. Extensive X-rays verified the spread of the disease. A lump had developed on my neck which the doctors had thought of removing, but when the X-rays revealed the extent of the disease, they decided not to touch the minor lump. Under the direction of our own family physician, we established a team of doctors, a neurosurgeon, a general surgeon, and a chemotherapist. They met and in consultation began to find methods of dealing with the situation.

Dudley and I established four principles for guidance in our relationship to the medical team: *first,* respect for my integrity as a person whose rational processes must be retained; *second,* no experimentation; *third,* use of every legitimate therapeutic process to relieve pain and/or facilitate chances of recovery; *fourth,* the ultimate decision rested with us, myself in particular, and not with the doctors. Following these principles, we faced together the most stupendous event which had ever confronted us. With calmness and realism we knew it was the imminence of my death.

Certainly the experiences and the crises of the past few years helped us face this. I determined not to pass the event of my death and funeral arrangements to anyone else if I could in good spirit be part of them. This mentality somewhat shocked my doctors, but I assured them that just as I had planned my wedding, the birth of the children, the wedding that had just taken place, I also felt it was my privilege, given time, to plan my own funeral. So we set about doing it. Again, the whole family shared this event, not in any catastrophic way, but in the reality of the eventual happening.

Dudley and I talked about the present crisis, the spread of disease.

"What thing takes precedence over everything else just now?" I asked Dudley, who turned and looked out of the window.

"Well, Alice, I guess it is your death."

"Well, then, Dudley, let's get to work and take care of that first. You bring pencil and paper to the hospital this evening, and we'll start working on a revision of our wills."

That evening he returned and we began marking down what I desired to have done with the few things I had. We took time to plan for the eventuality of Beverly's marriage within the next few years and the extra things she would need if I were not here to help her.[3] I carefully planned that she would have the same amount of money and the privileges that her sister had had.

As we settled each thing regarding the children, each came into the room and I carefully went over the plans. I talked with them freely and sometimes with a bit of humor about the plans and the part of the will that specially pertained to them.

After this Dudley and I talked about the funeral arrangements, the people I wished to take part in it, the message, hymns, pallbearers. We decided all those things and wrote them down under the guidance of our minister. The next question on our list: Where shall I be buried? Because of my birth-

---

[3] Beverly was married December 13, 1969, to David C. Reynolds of Raleigh, North Carolina, in a beautiful ceremony and with the vital spirit of Alice enlivening the entire preparation and the event. A further wonder was that Dianne, our elder daughter, carried in her body new life—an eight-month-old fetus—as she entered the chancel as matron of honor. Life moves on.

place in Canada and since I had not lived in any one place for long here in the United States, we even wondered about that country. This gave us an opportunity to face something we had never in any honesty confronted before. We talked about it with our children and decided that I would go back to my birthplace, to the family cemetery where we would purchase a plot. This decision in itself, strange as it may seem, lifted a great weight from our minds. We made arrangements for one of my brothers to purchase a plot, and within a few weeks all these things were done.

After finally settling the will and making all the arrangements for the funeral and burial, I said to my husband, "Now take all those papers home and put them carefully away; if within the next few days or months you must use them, all questions will be settled." Now we knew everything could be carried out in the best spirit with a knowledge that my desires would be fulfilled.

This brought an instantaneous freedom, as if many of my burdens which might have been projected into the family were lifted from our shoulders. I felt great relief that we had settled the business without morbidity.

These activities made one thing clear to me. Since the mastectomy, the word "cancer" must have brought the word "death" into Dudley's conscious mind through his subconscious mind. In some measure I was dead to him, I realized, although I didn't permit myself to speak about it in words. I know now that I did many things to prove I was the same person I had been before the operation. I know now both the futility of such attempts and the waste of energy. No one can prove to another person that she is alive if that other person has accepted, even for a moment, some degree of the other's death. Part of me had literally died for Dudley and, in many ways known and unknown to me, I reminded him of this death. My very presence often called forth within him this memory that he could not release for transmutation by the Holy Spirit. In spite of good intentions, he moved many times away from this thing that he had come to know as a threat to life as he desired it.

Dudley and I talked about this in the days when we took care of preparations for my actual death. Putting details down on paper, and talking about it with the family and minister, actually focused this fear of his; the actual confrontation of death destroyed this thing that had existed in his mind all these years.

I no longer tried to prove to him or anyone that I was alive, that the words "cancer" and "death" were not synonymous. The trauma of the situation forced us to admit it, and in some amazing way we were both set free. Neither of us realized it fully at the time, but it became increasingly clear in the days, weeks, months, and years since then.

After consultation, the doctors advised some minor surgery to remove the ovaries to stop the production of estrogen. The doctor came and talked to me about this. I agreed to the operation so long as it was sound medical practice. But I made it clear it was a therapeutic technique, and not an exploration to find a malignancy in my reproductive organs. I knew they did not have to do this operation because of suspected cancer in that area of my body. I had in previous years decided against such surgery because I knew it was not necessary—those organs of my body were healthy! On this basis, I submitted to surgery.

During the operation, the doctors also did an exploratory to determine the condition of the liver and the other organs surrounding it. I again had the experience of transcendence in this surgery just as I had in the surgery on my arm. I responded favorably after the surgery; in fact I do not recall having one gas pain or any uncomfortable experiences following it. It more or less became a minor detail; I had more important things to think about. Healing from the surgery came quickly, just a ripple along the way. However, the doctor who performed the surgery also confirmed the prognosis of no possible chance for recovery because the spread of cancer had encased the liver and the organs surrounding it.

One night, following a day of crisis, a special nurse cared for me. During the evening and the hours of the night, a flood of liquid waves of fire racked me, coursing through my body and breaking out on my skin. At that time they did not give me any medication that would soothe or relieve the pain. I turned to the nurse.

"Get some bath blankets in the cupboard in my room, and there you will also find a bottle of apple cider vinegar."

After a little argument, she realized I fully commanded the situation and knew that if she didn't do it, I would. When she finally got swabs and began to cover my body with vinegar, conditions began to change within my body, and I fell into a restful sleep. In the morning my doctor came.

"I hear that your room changed into a pickling factory last night."

"Well, was I wrong?"

"No, you were not wrong because you feel better this morning."

Thus I got along with very little medication. At first they thought I had to have certain pills every night to get my sleep. I convinced the doctor that I would have just as many hours of sound sleep with two tablespoons of honey as I would with the tablets they thought I must swallow every night. So they allowed me to use the honey instead of sleeping tablets. I suppose they figured I had only a short time to live anyway, so they might as well grant a few of the simple requests that a dying person makes.

The doctors, through very careful study and consultation, finally put me on three different drugs—dilanton, cortisone, and injection of a cancer drug. They carefully watched my body's reactions and took the blood count at necessary intervals.

I had a private room and set my own rules regarding that domain. I always graciously received and welcomed the doctors. My husband and my family would come at specified times and under certain conditions, not every day. While many visitors wanted to come, I did not permit this because I knew people were concerned and sympathetic, but usually did not know how to express their concern. Coming, although outwardly cheerful, into the hospital room, they would project this subconscious concern and sympathy for me, and those emotions were de-energizing and upsetting.

I talked with my minister, my husband, and family about death and life and what it meant to me. I talked to my doctors about the physical situation. I did not wish to engage in any discussion with just casual visitors or people not directly involved. A sign on my door stated "No Visitors." The same rules stood for the telephone—no calls into my room. If I had to call my family, or if they had to call me, that went through; no other calls were permitted. In this way I conserved energy. Many cards, letters, telegrams, and the endless flow of beautiful flowers all became elements of healing. Having flowers to care for in the morning, to arrange, to water, to love, provided tremendous source of strength and comfort—living things in my room, both day and night. I saw each as an expression of the bounty of God's love. They increased the power of God in the room.

One night in my sleep I saw an exquisite sweater in the most beautiful shade of blue. It attracted and delighted me so much that I found myself desiring it as something I knew I would like to have. I became aware of the thought that I should be given the sweater. After all, I had had so much taken from me; I had come through a great deal of suffering and pain. I almost thought the sweater would materialize for me. Someone would certainly give me this.

Then a voice said to me, "Why don't you knit it?" I replied to this voice, "Well, I haven't done any knitting for thirteen years." I reminded myself and the voice that the last time I had knit anything was the night before John was born. The voice again said, "An art once mastered is never lost. Knit this sweater." In the morning this dream remained an order I had to obey, a command within me to get a knitting book, needles, yarn, and start to knit.

I surprised Dudley with a call to his office and surprised him even more when I told him I wanted someone to go shopping for me. He thought my shopping days had ended, but he should have realized that unless he had me in the ground, I was going to find some way of going shopping here on earth! He put his secretary, Miss Jayne Crawford, on the line and I explained to her what I wanted to buy. She graciously went to the store for me and brought to the hospital a pattern, needles, and very beautiful yarn. While there, she helped me rethink the knitting techniques I had mastered many years ago, and together we got the sweater started.

People reacted differently when they caught me knitting. Both Dudley and the children took on a new attitude toward me: "Mother is knitting!" If someone asked Dudley about me, he would say, "Well, she's knitting." The response in itself drove back many of these depressing inquiries and analyses about my condition. Instead of asking me how I was, often my children would say, "Well, Mother, how much have you knit today?" Life began to take on a whole new dimension. As I knit, I also related to something beautiful, creative, and growing. The sweater became a conversation piece even for the doctors and nurses when they came into my room.

The crises receded, and by September 26 I went home in

time for our twenty-third wedding anniversary. Dudley and I decided that since our kitchen, library, dining room, and a bath were all on one level of our home, I could very well manage the work and family. For two weeks a kind friend insisted on bringing in our evening meal, but though this was a great blessing, within a short time we no longer needed this done for us.

During those weeks I enjoyed baking bread. I found in kneading the dough, in watching the yeast rise, inspiration and answers to some of the things for which I had searched. My first shopping came one day when my husband took me to a yard goods store where we selected some material for a new dress and a long skirt to wear to a dinner dance. This provided not only an opportunity for creativity and design, but an active anticipation of events.

I carried over into the home the disciplines that I had in the hospital regarding the telephone and visitors. My son and husband left for school and work before eight o'clock in the morning; until 4:30 p.m. I was largely alone. Very few visitors came, since the time limit was from five to ten minutes. This same rule pertained to the telephone. This necessary discipline helped me conserve energy, but was new for me and for many people who knew me through the years. For a long time I had carried on an active ministry through the home and the telephone. What a wonderful day when I could go outside in the garden and touch the flowers!

Everything seemed the same and yet different. The world outside was the same, but something profound had happened within me, as though I had been given a new, very tender life. I moved very slowly and carefully, knowing that many changes had to take place; changes I could not begin to comprehend. Actually I did not know many aspects of my new life, but had the assurance they would be revealed to me; the one thing required of me was obedience. I spent long hours just resting in silence, lying back in the arms of Christ, not trying to pray or to do anything, just abiding in the Christ. I didn't try to find out the why—the answers. The silence confirmed the awareness that the change had taken place within.

8 | CONFRONTING SOME
EMOTIONAL REALITIES

One day as I rested on the lawn I realized that the revelations I received brought two important events in my life into focus: my wedding and the wedding of our daughter Dianne. I recalled the days of preparation for her wedding when I had taken out a box containing articles from my wedding. They included my gown, veil, and trousseau articles; Dianne and I had recognized how radically styles change.

I felt the Spirit speaking to me about a situation I had found painful and had always tried to conceal. Dudley had requested in planning for our wedding that I ask his mother to make my wedding dress. Although I had reservations, I agreed to his request. I could not, at that time, have fully realized the depth of emotions regarding my marriage into his family. Understandably, such emotions were transferred into the dressmaking. I saw that the dress really did not symbolize our wedding joy. Now I began to understand that just as I had created difficulties by agreeing with him on its making, I also had kept it in my possession for the wrong reasons. This dress did not symbolize for me joy and happiness. I became strongly aware that I must deal constructively with this matter and all it stood for.

I felt motivated by unseen hands. I found myself getting a large can, placing it on the patio and starting a fire in it, going into the storage closet and reaching for the box. One by one, as I dropped the articles into the can, they caught fire and disintegrated, and something within me also dissolved. It seemed almost a ritual, and an internal freedom came that I had not known before in my married life. Guided to let the whole experience "go up in smoke," I did not mention it to anyone.

A few weeks later Dianne and her husband made their first visit home after their wedding. Sitting on the back steps listening to her recount the recent events of her new life, I found myself telling her what I had done.

"You know, it's strange but they were in shreds. I guess after twenty-three years of storage things do fall apart. I am not carrying any of these former things into my new life."

Dianne turned to me in amazed relief.

"Oh, Mother, I was afraid to come to see you. I've been wondering how I could ever tell you about the night during the wedding preparation that I got your things out of the storage closet and had them spread out when the telephone rang. I ran to answer the phone, and when I returned the pup had made shreds out of your things. I gathered up all the pieces and put the box back into its place. Later I told Dad what had happened, but he didn't want to be the one to tell you. So now the whole situation has been cared for. You've been set free from things of the past, both material and mental, and I've been relieved of my fears of telling you what I thought would be bad news."

This kind of cleansing went on day by day, quietly, without any big upheaval in our way of life, in our home, in my mental life, and in the deep levels of my subconscious and conscious mind. It became a turning from all forces negative, destructive, full of disease, and disharmonious, in whatever form they came—material, mental, and emotional. The total chemistry of my body and the balance of the elements that constituted my total well-being were at stake. So the change began and continued, and through periods of quietness, listening, and meditation, I learned of other things in the home with which I had to part—things once precious to me that now represented a wrong emotional force or desire. Some of these things I gave away to Goodwill Industries.

It was a very quiet cleansing. Weeks could go by and nothing would happen. Then I would know I had to remove certain things from the home because they were no longer part of my new life; I had no need of them. These things all related to myself, to my life—things I had thought important, some outward manifestations of wrong desires. Each time I obeyed the Spirit, I felt an uplifting, a rising of consciousness, as though a part of me had experienced a cleansing.

Whether I lived longer in this world or passed on to my life in the Spirit seemed irrelevant. I had to do certain things to attain the place where I could know spiritual healing. It included both mental and physical, my whole being moving toward a new creation. I only had to be faithful to my meditation and prayer life and obedient to the voice within—the voice of God. He knew what he willed to accomplish within me, even though my conscious mind could not understand the guidance that I was receiving at this particular time.

Many of the patterns and activities of my life began to change on the outer level as changes took place inwardly. I realized that forces such as fear, sympathy, and anxiety, coming from the outer world, could also be present in the inner circle of my family. These forces damaged me just as much if I permitted myself to relate to them, even if they involved family ties and a sense of responsibility. I could not live by two sets of values, one for my friends and persons who had come to me for help through the years and another for the inner circle of the family. God's will for my life did not include negative forces which hindered the healing from taking place. All the people were involved, not just those outside the family circle.

This deep therapy required an honesty that I had long tried to escape and cover up. The emotional body within me needed a center that could not be torn up or thrown out of balance by a phone call, letters, or communications from within the family circle about disease and disharmony. The fact that most of our relatives lived in Canada made no difference in regard to the emotional upheaval. Rather than becoming indifferent or uninterested in people, I had to relate to them in a new way. Through the years I had been drawn directly into the difficulties themselves. I seemed unable to discern elements of a healing nature in the situation and effectively relate to that.

In many of the situations in which I had become involved, by the time I got around to knowing the circumstances, others had begun to find answers and move toward a settlement. This left me depleted, de-energized, and with a real sense of resentment. I knew I could no longer afford such involvement, but the way to accomplish this change remained a mystery. A situation that had existed in my own family over a number of years helped to clarify my thinking.

One of my brothers, in the lumbering business, had been successful but was currently having some difficulty. One summer about thirteen years ago I visited him, saw the developing problem, and at that time became involved in helping him. I stayed through that summer, and when the time came for me to return to my U.S. home, no solution seemed apparent to the carrying on of the records. Thus we devised a system whereby I would continue to keep the records and we would send the information back and forth through the mails. I would make periodic visits to the lumber firm. This was a big responsibility because many times I would have to do this work after I had finished my house chores and put the children to bed. Often I would work late in the night.

Now I had to ask myself a difficult and recurring question: What are you relating to in this situation? I had to admit to myself for the first time in all these years that it was just not that I wanted to be a good sister or that I loved my brother, but that fear had motivated this work. I feared that my brother would fail, that the pressure would give him an excuse for drinking, which embarrassed me; that his records would get behind and the reports for the government would not be in the proper form. In essence, I related to the disharmony in his life.

Keeping his records was basically a mechanical thing which gave me satisfaction, but nothing had really changed visibly in the man himself or in his approach to life or his business. I was wrong to expect transformation on other levels. Perhaps one of the reasons why no changes occurred in his business was that he actually wanted my interest and relationship. He may have enjoyed having this relationship with no intention of making a change, because then he would lose my interest or involvement with him.

This relationship involved both creative and negative forces, but by being fearful and protective I had failed to face the issues directly with my brother that would have lifted this extra work from me and made him face his own responsibility. I further acknowledged that in my anxiety to keep everything straight I had involved my husband year after year because he is an accountant and did the final audit.

I asked myself: Have I been doing the right thing all these years for the wrong reasons? If I have been doing it out of fear and anxiety, then I have been relating to the same fear and anxieties within my brother that I had sought to transform through this work. I soon understood that the work in itself had no power whatsoever to transform anyone; that after all these years I must release the fear so that new patterns and new ways could be found.

I had to so stabilize the emotional center within me that it would not be thrown out of balance by such external happenings. Its quietness and strength operate through the Christ within.

I asked the Spirit again to reveal the negative forces to which I had related in the paternal family—fear, anxiety, and apprehension. Spirit is God, Spirit is Truth, and when the light shines upon a situation, it sometimes illuminates something we do not wish to see; but in the confrontation we must face the truth. My testimony now is that the Holy Spirit did move, and transformed inner emotions and outward expressions with the result that an entirely new base and development of this relationship toward my brother and other members of my family occurred.

I knew I was not just the type of person Dudley's family hoped he would marry. I had a different nature and background, definite ideas and strong determination. His mother and two sisters were very close, and Dudley represented many things that they desired—new adventure, new life, relationships on a higher social level with people of wealth and means. His early trips to New York and other places seemed exciting and brought a sense of adventure to the family. To this working-class English family he represented a new hope—something better than they had known. Thus almost any girl whom he would have courted at this time might have threatened them and the possibilities that they saw coming to them through him. They accepted me on the level of a person interested in Dudley's education and accomplishments. I knew this, but I could not face it and deal with it constructively at the time. I held a deep conviction that somehow my life was tied with Dudley's regardless of the obstacles in the way. We found joy in being with each other, talking, studying, and moving out

113

into the unknown. We would build our new life in another country, away from both families. I felt I could overcome these obstacles and win the love I desired from this family. However, I had much to learn about the mind and how it works in regard to emotions, resentments, and how to handle such forces. I could not discern the wisdom of my mother when she said, "Leave these family problems in Canada. Do not take them with you into your new life."

I took many things within myself and pondered them. I determined that nothing and no one would harm this marriage. I determined that everything else in life could go, but this one thing would be eternal, not only a success as the world would judge it, but also the purpose for which God ordained it. I also determined that I would not give the initiative to anyone in governing our life and that I did not want or require the love he should as a son and a brother give to his family. I would, I vowed, do all the things that the world said a good daughter-in-law should do and surely then a harmonious relationship would grow.

I stood in awe of their Fundamentalist Baptist religion, feeling hesitant to criticize or to evaluate it or them. A very long time passed before I understood their initial lack of real enthusiasm when Dudley made his decision to turn from the social and financial success that life offered him and enter the lowest rung of the Christian ministry, both on a social and financial scale.

This probably represented a keen disappointment to his family, especially the years we spent in the slums, when they compared that to the heights they saw him reaching prior to the marriage. I realize now my compulsion to be perfectly proper, even in the face of financial difficulties, about birthdays and other special days arose out of a great fear of getting into unpleasant verbal or emotional encounter. Always trying to safeguard myself against any further criticism, I knew I was failing at the same time.

In many ways our early relationships with his family became a matter of surface actions, niceties, pleasantries, and doing the right thing, but basically nothing changed in the emotions and desires. Yet I can honestly say that I kept on hoping for a change. As Dudley's career expanded in the church world and his social position and relationships began to move into a new level, with increased salary, the interest of his family increased in both his work and his life. This I recognized and welcomed, and we began to have through those years more visits and relationships with them.

After the life-and-death struggle, I could not do many things that I had done through the years to keep all the family relationships smooth and running. This reality had no place in it for subterfuge, and it didn't matter one iota whether people in or out of the families liked or disliked me; I had nothing more to prove in life. I had only one small thread to clutch. As I relinquished many things which I thought I had in my control, the Spirit began then to reveal the true conditions. The desire for a creative, loving relationship with my husband's family could never be granted on the basis of simply pleasing them.

I began to understand the teachings and actions of Jesus when he said a person must be separated from things and influences. I did not have to reject the person when I rejected the patterns of their thoughts and the imagery of their life. I wondered how I could constructively handle the good forces present in many situations between me, my husband, and his family. It became clear that I had to remove myself from the direct line of the emotions causing strain for my husband, a strain which often reached me through him. I realized at times when he could have seen the true situation, I was a shadow between him and the facts. Because I had permitted myself to be placed there, he grew accustomed to my being

115

there, and many times he passed the responsibility of ironing things out to me.

After my return home from the hospital I wondered how I could handle all these family relationships. I could no longer become involved when old patterns began to manifest themselves. Dudley thus came face to face with these realities and gradually perceived that persons are often misled and misunderstood as to essential realities, especially regarding the will of God. We began to know how destructive forces even in a potentially good relationship can operate and what we must do to eliminate them.

I knew I had capitulated to forces I did not understand at the time, and forces I knew not how to handle. When the Spirit drew the circle smaller, I recognized the fact that Dudley was a part of the Ward family, both by birth and nature. I could not deny who and what, nor could I by any act of will or dedication to him or our life transform these forces within him myself. The Spirit of God moving on his spirit must work them out. When the Spirit began to move on this level within me, the fears and anxieties that prompted much of my former endeavors were eliminated.

I knew that the forces which had often prevailed were contrary to the creative power and will of God. God's nature and the laws of the universe always move toward wholeness of life in physical, mental, and social relationships. It is not in the absence of problems that we find the answers to life, but rather in the confrontation of such problems we learn what forces and elements of life are involved, and know a higher control. When I realized that I did not confront personalities alone but rather a state of minds, I began to comprehend new dimensions and to gain wisdom in dealing with these problems.

For a number of years as the Holy Spirit began to work with all of us, we began to see great changes taking place. The two wider families—the Armstrongs and the Wards—came into-closer communication. Dudley's father and my mother came to appreciate each other deeply. My own relationship with Father Ward, a very wonderful man—Dad, as we called him—became very close. So much a reality is he in the spirit world following his death a few years ago that he is a frequent and happy visitor in our home. Dudley and I both became extremely sensitive to his presence and his great delight. He often came in the company of both my mother and father. Dudley's mother struck up a wonderful, creative, and healing friendship with the brother whom I have referred to previously. My own relationship to Mother Ward—Mom, as we called her—Dudley's sisters, and his brother became a warm and loving one. Two practical things were especially influential in the growing fondness between Mother Ward and me. One was, we both developed a great interest in prayer and prayer groups. The other was sharing my clothes with her. I sent her several times a year a box of carefully selected and good clothes with which she was delighted and for which she was so grateful. As a matter of fact, it developed that she wore practically only my clothes.[1] Dianne's wedding and our twenty-fifth wedding anniversary were events which provided beautiful evidence of the growth and healing which had taken place among all these strong people.

Another revelation came as I went to the hospital for my blood tests and then to my doctors for continued chemical therapy. These technical procedures held no cure, but were the

---

[1] One of the most unusual things happened at the time of Alice's funeral in Madoc, Canada (see Epilogue). Just two days before her passing Alice packed two boxes of clothes—one for some nieces and nephews in Canada, the other a large box of especially precious and unique clothes, which Alice herself had made from cloth Dudley purchased in the Far East, for Mother Ward. When Mother Ward returned from Alice's funeral, waiting at her door was the package. She was overwhelmed at the significance and wonder of this event. God is very good.

only procedures available to me on the scientific and technological level. I knew another dimension of experience and expression must come to me. I realized that my mother, as she spoke to me a few weeks before she died, had given me the truth in our last telephone conversation.

"Alice, you have something to give the world and you can never give it to Dudley or through him to the world as Alice Ward. It must be given through your real self."

I began to search for some meaning to this message. Who am I? What did I have to give? Was I really afraid of the church or Dudley's position in the church? If I were to speak out on some of the things that I had experienced through the Spirit, would the world think me queer? Would I be rejected because of the spiritual gifts that had been given to me? Or was I afraid people would use these gifts for inferior goals?

Another thread became entangled in the pattern of our lives over a period of years and threatened our personal and family security. This resulted from the emotional involvements, constructive and destructive, in work and with persons related to it. As Dudley became more deeply immersed in his work, especially during times of stress, he failed to see the hazard with which the intensity of his involvement threatened the happiness and harmony of myself and the family, and began to separate his relationships and loyalties into compartments. Dudley compounded the problem by a protective attitude toward the personal relationships of his work.

He rationalized all of this nicely without fully realizing that he was putting his wife and family into one setting, and outside interests, particularly his work, into another. The righteousness of the vocation often prohibited sound questioning and objective evaluation. Only as you pass through a prolonged period of stress can you become aware of the different factors feeding into it. Any one factor taken alone could, in all likelihood, be handled without too much effort. When compounded, they also are hidden and hard to untangle.

The almost unknown, the least suspected, line of stress actually may be the most persistent and threatening. This is due frequently to the fact that you refuse to recognize the stress for what it is, and the subtle ways you add to it, probably because you may not know how to handle it or really don't want to. When you attempt to submerge, rather than to surface, difficulties, they tend to increase and build up. Often such problems come in disguised and righteous dress and in forms that appear good, especially within the church, when in essence they are destructive and disease laden.

This can become most confusing to a person who thinks he is trying to live by the motto "See no evil, hear no evil, speak no evil." You can feel guilty even in suspecting the source of the stress. For a time you may even close your eyes, thinking a person is not really doing what obviously he is doing. You may begin to believe that such problems will just go away. But they invariably become more real and your uncertainty tends to feed into them. The same principle is relevant there as in all of life. We have found so often in our search that you must know what to deny and what to affirm within yourself before you can change the outer situation. Healing must begin at the center of our beings.

Learning in this area is costly and slow. The possibilities of emotional and physical separation and rejection between two people are real, especially when other persons and events are so present and absorbing. One of the real hazards in such a situation is self-pity. For example, you may harbor the persistent thought that somewhere, somehow, you have failed as a wife and companion. You consider many of the suggested gimmicks, but know somehow they will have little effect. You must seek for deeper cause and meaning.

In most vocations or work relationships when you become

aware of such difficulties, you can find ways to relieve them, but when related to the church, you face an added set of problems. People expect ministers and their wives to give guidance, help, and counsel to the community, but to be apart and above these happenings. This is an unrealistic position, limits the true growth of the persons, and is false to our role in dealing with people and their needs.

However, awareness of a source of personal and family stress is quite different from ability to handle it as a wife and mother. I realized I was confronting deep desires, emotions, thought patterns, and an energy about which I knew little. My search to understand was very much a part of my need for wholeness. I knew of no one to whom I could go for help. So I sought this help through prayer and communion with God. To my physical needs was added the awareness of forces beating against my inner life. Gradually I received direction on what to read and study for enlightenment. I saw that my fear within needed to be healed before I could handle it externally. I entrusted all of this for prayer by those whom I had grown to respect.

Through a release, which came from the strengthening power of fellowship, I began to find freedom and to relate to constructive things in my daily life and relationships. I began to experience the dissolving of fears within me and to discover the true nature of others. Pride, position, work, other people, the family and marriage were all part of it, but I was central in it all. Only when I faced the reality that the self within me was threatened did I start to receive direction. I knew I was dealing with a basic principle of life and with forces which deplete the person. Squarely before me stood the question of my true security. What was being threatened? This called forth from me a new depth of love, not of myself, and out of this I began to make decisions. I realized that no amount of talking would open Dudley's eyes as to how his intense involvement and protectiveness of everything about his career affected him. This would only come in his own time of enlightenment when he himself would be ready to receive.

My guidance indicated I should tend to my own illumination. Thus I began, through the Spirit, to learn how to reject fear and to affirm the power and goodness of God present within me. With it came a new consciousness of authority. I had to deny those things in my life contrary to the Spirit of Christ from within my own consciousness before external change would occur. I knew that a cleansed subconscious could no longer attract forces that contribute to stress. At such a time the home should not be a haven into which one retreats, nor the family completely consuming. Rather, both should be securities out of which one moves. The home became a center and a stronghold of prayer power and increasingly centered in God. Not until then did I begin to realize how much tension I had taken into myself. I desired freedom from the presence of stress because I knew it was damaging my physical, mental, and spiritual health.

I began to thank God for a deeper healing and for the wisdom revealed to me in my search. When you begin to loose fears and to find the center being stabilized within, a cleansing gratitude flows. In this spirit you can pray for the same release and good to come to others. In giving thanks, you are saved from the temptation to judge and condemn, realizing that God does not, and you dare not.

Slowly you grasp the truth that what is feared has no power of itself, only the power your thoughts give to it. You no longer rely entirely upon any one human relationship for your security. Life is much more than one individual, even a husband or wife, and love cannot be limited in that way. As I began to know true thankfulness for the lessons learned and the perceptions gained, I was set free for a new transcendent consciousness of God and love for my fellowmen. Slowly the picture changed. Old images

121

passed away and I experienced a new authority in an obedience to a love and a law higher than I had known before.

Dudley, caught in the midst of this and increasingly open to the work of grace, slowly began to experience a new perspective on his life, work, ministry, and relationships. He began to see justifiable expectations in his work and the margins beyond which other persons, and even the church, could not bind him or expect from him an effort which blinded him to the needs of his total life. He knew that in the exhausting demands of his work he had at times demanded too much of all concerned, both family and work colleagues. When these insights finally became a reality, the meaning of his life and work came into sharper focus. Pressures were relieved, events began to occur, and changes in relationships took place which contributed to the good of all.

Perhaps our elder daughter best expressed the values that held us to a principle greater than ourselves in letters to us on Mother's Day and again on Father's Day in 1967.

Dear Mother,

It would be difficult for me to put into words adequately all I feel for you and all that you have and do mean to me. But somehow I think I should try.

The days when you used to make us wear leggings and take our vitamins, eat good food, get enough rest, do our homework, and take care of our chores have passed. They weren't always the easiest of days or years, but they were essential. And I see even more so now why they were so important in shaping our habits, character, and lives.

If this was all you had done, I would still think of you as an excellent mother. But, you as a person are so much more than just someone who cared for my physical needs. I'm beginning to realize now just what it means to have someone like you for my mother. You are a very special person and a very special friend. You have such deep insight into, and sensitivity for, the very basis of life itself. And, although I cannot begin to fully comprehend your faith or the full scope of your experience, just being exposed to your type of love has made my life richer and more meaningful.

When Mike and I were shopping one day, we ran into ————. We chatted casually and then he happened to mention a letter you had written to him. He said that when he feels at his lowest, he takes your letter and rereads it often. It somehow gives him just what he was looking for and makes each particular situation seem easier to handle and face. He said he feels very honored to know you and that you are one of the finest people he has ever met.

I know what you've meant to Mike. I see the way he looks when he tells other people about how wonderful you and the things you do are—as he often does! He believes in you, though perhaps does not know precisely why. Though, for him, just knowing and loving you seems to be sufficient. It is hard to explain how I feel when I realize the person that so many people admire and love is my mother. Mainly, I suppose, I group myself with them. When I have had problems and have turned to you, I've found the guidance and strength I needed. The unconscious and conscious feeling of knowing that there is someone who is constantly praying for and thinking of you is one of the most precious experiences of my life. I, too, am honored to know you; I, too, believe in you and in your work. You are a very special gift, and your constant and unselfish love is one of the dearest treasures I possess.

Mike has said that I love too hard. I know you'll understand when I say that there is often a physical ache attached to that kind of love. However, it is one of the wonders of life that there are persons like you and Daddy, who can call forth that kind of love from another person.

And so on Mother's Day, I write to you in a very humble and slightly disorganized way to tell you again that you are one of the

123

most precious parts of my life—and, were you not my mother, I'd ask only that you be my friend.

Dianne—1967

Dear Dad,

   It looks like this is my year for writing letters. I suppose it's because I feel somewhat like I'm on the other side of the globe. Missing you, of course, makes me think of you more, though it does much more than that. Especially in the last few months I've realized that no matter how many miles separate us, I'm never really that far away. I know, however, how important this feeling was in my childhood. For, with you traveling so much as you did, it was essential for us to realize that no matter where you were, we were still a close-knit family group. I know, also, how very important to me were your unspoken rules and unwritten goals— those which I accepted as guidelines for so many of my activities. Whether I realized it then or not, <u>I know now that trying to gain your approval was one of the motivating forces in my life at home.</u> I knew you loved me—even after one of your memorable spankings! When you'd come and sit at the edge of my bed, no matter how much I thought I "hated" you, you'd manage to make me cry when I began to realize that you had indeed "done it for my own good"—you were asking me to measure up! I knew you loved me when we used to take our evening walks in Illinois. By asking a myriad of questions, I learned so much. And I knew you loved me on the Valentine's Day of my sophomore year at Emory. That beautiful day will always remain as one of the loveliest memories of my life. But more than loving me, I wanted you to be proud of me. I knew I was proud of you—proud of your intelligence and position, proud that some found you too outspoken and controversial, proud that you were respected and admired by so many others. I hope you know how deeply important it was for me to be proud of my parents—not for what we had in the way of possessions, but what we had as family and friends.

Ultimately, I think what has made me the proudest is the way in which you and Mother have taken Mike into our family and deep friendship. He is so proud to call you his friend and, in turn, wants you especially to be proud of him. In the past few years I have found great happiness in realizing that, in addition to loving your daughter, you also missed her. The way in which you say good-bye when someone is leaving (in your quick and almost offhand manner) is not as it appears to be. And, when you actually said on the phone a few weeks ago that you missed having us around, well, I cried when we hung up, but I was so happy to realize that I could be missed. This is so very important to one member of such a close family who marries and moves away. I, of necessity, have to move into a somewhat different relationship with my family, but to lose the precious parent-child relationship would be unbearable. This may sound overly dramatic, but it is nevertheless true.

And thus, on this Father's Day, I send all my love to a very successful father and a wonderful person! You are both to me, and happily are, as you've said, "cut from a different cloth" than most. How fortunate I am to be your daughter.

Dianne—1967

Some families have a heritage not of one generation's making, and it must be preserved and passed on at all costs. This is why, more than for just obvious reasons, one would preserve the sanctity of marriage, the home and family. It is the divine freedom within the relationships that would protect and deny anyone, anything, or any institution possession. The good marriage is not one of complete bliss, but one in which the overcoming of problems has developed a greater love. Often the more subtle things of the mind separate and destroy a union. When this happens, from whatever causes, harmony is threatened. In a healthy marriage each one must move toward

125

increased ability to handle wisely the daily problems and not to an increase of bondage or exploitation. Dudley and I discovered through inner suffering we could only realize this as we found the Christ and made him the center of our lives and King of its various parts.

9 | EMERGING SPIRITUAL INSIGHTS

For almost nine months I was treated with the cancer drug. This meant that each Monday morning I went to the hospital for blood tests. Reports on the tests went to my doctors, and Wednesday morning I went to his office to receive the report and the injection. I followed this routine until June, 1966, when I began to realize my system was reaching a saturation point on the drug. This realization came as an inner knowing and a sensitivity for which I had no scientific backing, so I did not feel capable of speaking to my doctor. In my prayer period and contemplation regarding this, I sensed that the only direction was to wait until this manifested itself in my physical body. At that time I would know there was no need for alarm, and I would move through this crisis in the way others had come and gone.

On one of my September visits to the doctor's office, he gave me an injection which became the test one. The arm, at the point of injection, within a few hours became inflamed, feverish, and swollen. John, my son, and I were home alone at this time, and since it was evening, we didn't disturb the doctor, but I started a medication of warm castor oil which we rubbed into the arm. We kept hot towels around the arm, and propped it up into an elevated position with a number of pillows. John rubbed the castor oil into my arm and brought hot compresses to the bed, so that the medication continued through the evening and at intervals all through the night. I experienced quite severe pain up the neck and in the head area where I had had previous difficulty. By morning both the swelling and fever had subsided and I went to my doctor for consultation. He could see the inflamation that had set in. I asked, in the light of this, that the chemotherapist and the neurosurgeon review my case.

In a few days they called and said they would like me to consider another drug. I would take it orally. They did not contemplate starting it for a few weeks and frankly told me about the effects of the drug—the loss of my hair.

As I hung up the phone and began to think of the possibilities confronting me, it seemed as though I held in my hand again the choice of a few more months of life and the demand to give up something. Never until then did I begin to realize what my hair meant to me and what it represented in my life. When I sat down to pray and consider this new drug, I found I could not focus my attention on it at all. It was not the paramount thing. My whole attention was consumed with the loss of hair. I had to face honestly what my hair meant to me, not just now at the present time, but all of my life. I had largely taken for granted my hair and its beauty.

I was born with naturally curly hair, and fifty years ago that was considered a great blessing. My first memories include those of the pride of my family, especially my parents, over my long curls. My hair drew attention and comments from people. I would have to stand for long periods having my hair brushed, combed, and curled as Mother carefully perfected every curl. Sometimes it seemed like an endurance contest. Often I did not like stopping my play to have my hair combed, but it did set me apart and gave me special attention in our large family. I was conscious in a childish way that they were proud of my hair and not just me.

One warm summer's day when I was about five years old, I expressed my rebellion. I went to the barbershop in my small town in Canada and convinced the barber to cut off all my curls. I knew I could convince him because I brought along a brown paper bag in which to carry the curls home. I remember that he put a board across the armrests of his barber chair, hoisted me up, and put a cloth around me. I'll never forget the first sharp snap of the scissors and the curl that dropped from my head. As the other curls dropped on the floor, I had a feeling of emancipation. I scampered down from the chair and gathered them up, put them in my brown paper bag, and told the man that Daddy would come by to pay him. Then I started up the street toward my father's blacksmith shop. I stood in the doorway as I had done many times, and waited for him to notice me. He came out from under a horse he was shoeing and looked across to where I was standing and then he moved slowly closer to me. As he came near me, I saw tears on his face and all he said was, "Alice, you better go home."

I started up the street toward my home and I remember how people stopped and said, "What happened to you? What did you do with your curls? Where are they?" I held up the paper bag and said, "They are all in here, I had them cut off." I remember vividly feeling the freshness of the cool air around my neck and the freedom from the weight of the curls hanging from my head.

My mother's, brothers', and sisters' shock matched my father's when I appeared in the doorway. I remember that night as an unhappy one for my family. It was as though something beautiful they cherished had been lost. I remember the neighbors coming and talking with my mother. I sat alone on the steps trying to understand all that was going on. I did not feel any condemnation or any guilt about it. I really felt good. I just had one desire—to make my hair straight—and so began my struggle to change my hair myself. I would use a lot of water and try to slick it down, but I found to my great distress that when the water dried my hair would have even more curl. This became a very frustrating experience for a little girl.

My sister Anne, two years younger than I, had straight hair, and I wanted my hair to be like hers, but no matter what I did, my hair would curl. This continued to be the envy of my sister and my friends through my initial school years. Then came the invention of permanent waves and means whereby people with straight hair could change their hair into curly hair. Now my sister could have curly hair if she chose; my friends could have curly hair, and I no longer was set apart as a favorite of God. I thought that this would make my sister and me alike and we would both have curly hair. Although I failed to achieve straight hair like hers, she could have curly hair like mine and then everything would be right between us.

But this did not happen. No matter what we did, no matter how hard through these fifty years my sister and I tried to achieve a happy relationship, something stood between us, and both of us instinctively knew it. We tried in many ways during this period to overcome the block. I seemed to bring to her consciousness some memory that prohibited harmony between us.

Now, in the struggle for life itself, I faced the loss of my hair. I cannot put into words the agony of this possibility. I truly felt the Lord had gone too far this time when he touched even my hair. Surely this one thing I could have. This bitter struggle went on for over a week, and one evening as I sat at the dining room table, I heard a voice.

"Go into the drawer where you keep the family pictures and get the one taken first, when you were about four years old and Anne was about two, and find the one taken the next year, while you still had your long, curly hair."

As I looked at these pictures, I understood one source of the difficulty between us these many years. It was my hair. There in the little children's pictures I saw it. I sat on a chair with my long curls and a big lovely hair ribbon; my sister stood beside me with her plain straight hair. I recalled the time spent in preparation for the trip to the photographer, my mother brushing, combing, and curling my hair. My sister must have watched this procedure and envied both the attention and the time spent on me, possibly even the big starched ribbon attached to my hair. This childish resentment showed even at the age of two, even though she didn't know that such an emotion existed. Her eyes had this same expression a year later when we had our pictures taken. I began to understand the emotion which we had tried, each one in her own way, to dissolve through all these years.

When I saw this and realized the deep desire within my heart to have a good relationship with my sister, I sank to the floor and asked the Lord to take away my hair if that were the price to pay to have this separation ended. I thanked God that he was going to do it. In the days that followed I felt this was being accomplished through the love of God in the hearts of both my sister and myself.

One evening the telephone rang and it was a call from Canada. My sister insisted that I tell her about my current therapy and the drug I was taking. I found myself telling her about the new drug and that when I started it, I would likely lose my hair.

"It's not important that you have hair, Alice; it is important that you live." Somehow, at that moment, I knew that she was seeing me, not as she had seen me all these years, as a person whom God blessed with curly hair, a symbol of special attention and envy, but as a person, losing my hair; so the image changed. Her desire for me to live became paramount in her mind, and it dissolved the other envy and resentment and all the emotions over which she had no control in the formative years of her life. As this release became a reality within me, I turned in prayer to God and asked him for guidance on the drug.

I released this confrontation to two other people for prayer, one in America and a friend in England. The guidance came strongly that I should not take this drug at this particular time. I told the doctor of my conviction regarding this drug and he suggested another drug to me. I asked for more time to pray about my taking this particular drug. Three weeks later I went to see my chemotherapist, and after a complete examination, we sat together in his counseling room. My complete record lay before him and he went through it, reading it carefully. Then he very quietly asked me what instruction I had received in my prayer about this drug. In complete respect and understanding, I told him about my experience and what God had revealed to me. I had received no direct command as I had on the other drug. Rather, God put this drug, as it were, on the sidelines. It was present, it was there, it was acknowledged for its worth and the good it had done, but in no way or at no time did it move toward me. After a period of quietness in his office, the doctor spoke very calmly.

"Mrs. Ward, then that's where it is going to stay regarding you. It is the kind of drug you have been told about, and all of the good things about it are true; there are also many things that are unknown about it. Our scientific knowledge of many of these things is very small and I am not about to go against your guidance. In my thorough examination of your body today, I can find no evidence of the progress of disease or of the tumors. If tomorrow you were to come into my office for an examination and I were to find such evidence, the only drug that, at this time, I would advise giving you is this drug. But as you are asking us for nothing in the way of medication, then we can be frankly honest with you and tell you the truth. If you were to ask me for a drug today, this is the drug I would advise giving you. You have asked for nothing and are content to leave this drug where I think it should be, where God placed it in your consciousness—on the sidelines. So we will hold it in case any day we may need it in your therapy."

As my physical body increased in strength, and I began to take on wider responsibilities, I became aware that my need for the Holy Sacrament had increased, as though the Communion I received in the chapel of our church on Sunday morning could not sufficiently sustain my body and my ministry to others during the week. This related to my whole body, not only the spiritual, but the physical and mental as well. It was also at this time that fasting presented itself to me as both a means of grace and a method of cleansing.

Thus I began to go with Dudley, as often as he was in town, to the Washington Cathedral (Episcopal), within easy driving distance from our home, for Communion at 7:30 each Tuesday morning. Following the service, I fasted for the next twenty-four hours. As a rule I spent this day at home doing regular housework, perhaps seeing one person in the afternoon for consultation and preparing the evening meal for the family. The disciplines of this day reminded me of the source of my inner spiritual help. The need for spiritual food through the Communion was evident. I also saw that my physical body needed both time and means to flush the residue of drugs from the system. During the fast I drank water with a little lemon juice and a teaspoon of molasses in it. The discipline also served the purpose of denying myself indulgences.

Alone for so much of the time over a period of many months, I could have easily substituted food for the restricted activities. This would have intensified a problem I faced in taking the drugs which resulted in an increase in fluid weight from five to ten pounds above normal. I did not add to that problem by overeating. I learned to prepare and serve food to my family for their enjoyment, while at the same time denying myself. On this day of fasting I did not withdraw from my family; instead, I was very much present in preparing and serving the meal, and I stayed with them during the eating time. They recognized and respected my decision. Mealtime in our home was more than just the food. It was also a communion in relating the events of the day, new ideas, and laughter.

I began to recognize the many stages in my evolving understanding of Holy Communion. The early years of catechism in the Presbyterian Church and the requirements of being able to recite this before the elders of the church, before receiving my first Communion, were revived in memory. I recognized that by becoming a Methodist I placed a different importance on Communion. Often in the churches we served, we observed the sacrament at eight o'clock on Sunday morning for those who wished to come. Both Dudley and I believed that our congregation should have Communion regularly. I knew Communion was an important part of my healing. I learned through discipline and denial that Communion was more than receiving the elements. It was also a willingness to be present in Communion with other sufferers, an understanding that all relationships, if of a healing nature, must be lifted out of the self into the living Christ present in Communion and in my fellowman. In coming to the Communion, I was putting myself in relationship to Christ and the needs of others, where I could both receive and be used in the ministry of the Spirit. I realized that in seeking healing for my own pain and suffering, I would receive it to the degree that I came into healing relationship with the pain and suffering of the wider community. I knew, too, that in being healed, I would be released to something greater within myself.

My heels on the marble floor of the National Cathedral have sounded so noisy in the early morning that I often felt like taking off my shoes. I have been almost overwhelmed by the vastness and the beauty of the structure and have felt so insignificant as I walked through the different sections to get to the chapel for the services. This service was especially meaningful at Easter, 1967, when I went for the first time to Resurrection Chapel, a smaller chapel down in the lower part of the Cathedral.

Some mornings only two or three persons would participate in the Communion, never anyone that I knew personally. Going to the Cathedral for this early morning service, I was positioning myself for confession and for receiving the nourishment which I believe my spiritual body required. At times the desire to receive the elements grew so intense within me that I experienced an impatience with all the ritual. Then I would have to speak to my soul to bring it into obedient relationship to the spirit of the service. The desire within and the factors without had to come into synchronization before I knew the reality of the Living Presence of Christ. When I came into this realization of oneness, it seemed that the Risen Christ was everywhere present and I was continually hearing his word.

"Alice, behold I am All in All, in everything, all the reading, the prayers, candles, flowers, window, the immense columns that hold up the structure, and most of all in the priest who celebrates, and the people who kneel at the altar with you."

I saw the Christ. He was like a light that moved from one person or object to another, penetrating, illuminating, lighting everything from within, and involving the great oneness of the universe. The limitless light was present in the smallest particles. But there was no great and small because wherever this light moved, everything was illumined. Everything was there now. I no longer felt alone in the vastness of the Cathedral, with only a few people present. Suddenly it was all part of me and I was part of it. We belonged together in the wonder and mystery of creation itself. The Christ within me would continue to reveal himself to me in new and amazing ways. I was to behold him, and to see him in everything and obey his voice. There was a fullness to life, and if I neglected one aspect, I would weaken all of it.

Holy Communion and the Sacrament of Healing were part of the All I had witnessed in the moving light. They are not separate; they are part of the whole. As I experienced the immensity of the Christ, present in even one object or one person, I knew he was present in all of life, waiting to be recognized and to burst forth into fuller life. I felt a living, vital part of this vastness. I was not overwhelmed in the least by it, but rather I walked in it and with it. It was all present within me and somehow moving with me.

One morning while I was waiting to receive the elements, a person in light appeared before me. He placed in my out-stretched hands a bunch of blue forget-me-nots. As he did, I heard the words, "Alice, forget me not." The Presence re-mained there as I received the elements, and only disappeared as I rose to leave the altar. The command and the vitality of the Presence and the flowers remained with me, and I sought for the truth in it. I saw a living Presence, radiant, and that which he placed into my keeping was also alive, with form, color, and identity.

Had I out of my pain and suffering, in coming to the Lord's Table, identified myself with his pain and suffering, rather than his victory over pain and suffering? Was I unconsciously hold-ing on to some form of suffering in my mistaken desire to be like him? In coming to Communion did I bring with me the realization of the crucified Christ or the Risen Lord? If it were the crucified Christ, then I was identifying myself with him in my pain and suffering and a part of me was holding to it. I was not relinquishing it for cleansing and healing, because I thought it was part of Christ.

In the vision of the Presence and the flowers I came to see that I should identify with the Risen Lord and living substance to be raised with him and set free from pain and suffering. The victory was in the Risen Christ, in living substance; it was this life force within me that motivated me to come to the Communion table, rather than the presence of pain and suffering. As this living presence within me received the elements, my physical body was thereby cleansed and fed. This substance entered into the cells of my being, cleansing and supplying the proper chemical balance. My bloodstream was part of a greater circulatory system of the whole body of the Living Christ. The words of Paul, "I live, yet not I, but Christ liveth in me," became a living reality in my own body.

Then I could see the disease which threatened to take my life as a condition that required medical care and treatment, but not as an entity in itself. It had to decrease in the re-creation that was taking place within my body. I began to ask myself how I could best cooperate with an organ such as the liver, to know healing and wholeness. What could I eat or do to assist in this process, not only for the internal organs, but also for the recalcification of the outer layer of the skull? During the recent crisis, the cancer had spread to my skull, making parts of it like sponge. But in this healing light and life it was steadily recalcifying, and within a year was completely so. This is victory.

I sought information in many books, through prayer, and through listening. I experimented and gradually learned of foods that would blend in giving the needed substance. This was part of the Communion experience and a means by which I worked daily with the creative forces within me. In this research study and action, I related to the Christ-consciousness within me, and communed with him.

Seven years had elapsed since the former crisis which the children shared; in 1965 they were again faced by another. Their growth and maturity can be illustrated in three instances that pertain to each one individually.

Dianne, twenty-one, had just married and was experiencing her first adventure in establishing her own home. She was not in Washington during the crisis, but expressed her spirit and concern in a little prayer she wrote and sent to me:

A SPECIAL PRAYER

Hold her gently in Thy hands,
With love and warmth and tender care;
Hold her closely in Thy arms,
That she may find quiet comfort there.

September 7, 1965

She did not just write this, but inscribed it on a beautiful card, which she painted. Through it I knew the heart of my child, and I felt a unity with her spirit.

Beverly, nineteen, busy getting ready to go to college, was part of the daily events and the trips to and from the hospital with her father. One night as she completed a full day's work in the home by some ironing, she sat down at the kitchen table, feeling lonely and burdened by the entire course of events. Suddenly she heard something hit the kitchen window. She got up and saw a little bird hanging by just a claw to the window sill. The impact of hitting the window had been so great that the bird was quivering all over.

As she looked at the bird, she was torn between standing there to watch, or running down to the garden to prevent his fall, or to somehow pick him up when he fell. Transfixed by what she saw, she could not move from the spot and was amazed to see another little claw come up and touch the window sill. Gradually he fastened both his claws on the window sill, and as he began to stabilize himself, the quivering in his body subsided, and slowly he grew calm and still. Then he turned his head.

138

"He looked right at me, and at that moment of contact, he spread out his wings and flew away into the night," Beverly said.

For awhile she just stood there looking out into the night, and then she realized that her mother would do the very same thing. Although she now hung only by a slender thread, gradually she, too, would be stabilized, gradually the convulsive quivering and the moment of crisis would subside, she would again get her balance, and with a clear vision she would fly again. This experience so lifted her spirits that she completed her ironing and other work that night with a sense of joy and confidence. Early the next morning she called the hospital.

"Mother, I have good news."

"Oh Beverly, tell it to me."

"No, I must come to see you. When can I come?"

As soon as the attendants prepared the room and I was ready to receive her, Beverly came into my room. Her face was radiant, truly beautiful, filled with life and hope. She sat down beside my bed.

"Mother, I just don't want you to think I'm foolish, or that this didn't happen, because it really did, and I know it is true. The message is true and I want to tell it to you."

Then my daughter related the incident of the little bird, what it meant to her, and what she believed it was going to mean to me. Beverly left that day for college and did not come home again until Thanksgiving. As she and I walked to the grocery store to buy the turkey for our dinner, she turned to me.

"Mother, the little bird was right, wasn't it? That little bird knew that during all of these weeks in college when I would get afraid and wonder what was happening, or what was going to happen, I would either hear or see a bird or I would recall that the little bird knew everything was going to be all right and my mother would spread her wings and fly again. Here we are walking together to the grocery store, and the bird knew. I guess it was just God's way of telling me that I should have faith instead of fear."

Johnny was thirteen, a sensitive age for a boy, an age in which one changes, so that the many things he did for me in the previous illness did not come naturally now. But after I had come home from the hospital, one day he said he had a sore throat and thought he should not go to school. I said, "All right, John, we'll check it." His father was out of town for the entire week, and I knew that he had a deep sense of responsibility for me. We did many things that week. We played games —checkers, chess—on the floor together, watched television, read books, and all the time I knew that this boy's throat was not really so sore that he could not go to school. He just had to know that I was really home again, and he wanted to be with me. He wanted to absorb the fact.

I also knew that this child wanted to tell me something, something about those weeks of crisis that he had lived through too, and what it meant to him now. Our dining room is on the second floor and has two large glass doors looking out into a lovely garden and park. Gradually, toward the end of the week he asked me to come there to lie down with him.

"Mother, have you ever just watched the sky? Have you ever looked into the sky and thought you saw something? You know, when you were away, many times I came in here and just lay down and looked at the sky, and somehow or other I would always see something wonderful, and sometimes when I was waiting for the bus and didn't know what was going to happen that day, I would look up into the sky and sometimes I saw beautiful things there, and my day would change. It would be a good day for me. I would like you to just watch the sky with me for awhile and see what we can see."

So we played the game, my John and I, though I never could see all the things he saw. I did see some things, and we had a good time. Then one day I knew John would tell me the thing he wanted to say so much.

"Mother, when everybody else was afraid and thought you were going to die, I wasn't afraid at all, because I knew something. I knew that you were too strong to die, and that you will never really die because of the strength within you."

After a few moments of quietness, John jumped up, went upstairs, took off his pajamas, put on his clothes, and ran out the door; the sore throat disappeared. He was well because he had shared with me that which he had held deep within him— the faith of a boy of thirteen. I believe in the faith, not only of this child, but the faith of Beverly, as she accepted the message of a little bird, the faith of Dianne, who expressed it in art and print as she transcribed onto paper the prayer of her heart. These great expressions of my children, living in reality, showed a maturity that was in itself a deep, growing experience. Each one was involved, and yet each one in his or her own way, and for all of us, found a transcendence which gave a victory to each and to all.

10 | AND SO THERE WERE TWENTY-FIVE

September, 1967, our Silver Wedding Anniversary, twenty-five years of life together, brought many of the diverse elements that make for celebration, joy, realization, true family and friends, adventure, crisis, and freedom. Dudley and I planned to make it, with God's help, a wonderful month. On the first weekend of the month we went to Canada to complete the final plans for a reunion with our families. Later in the week all the living brothers and sisters and their children over fourteen years old from both families, and Grandmother Ward, the only living grandparent, gathered for a dinner and dance at the Quinte Hotel in Belleville, Ontario.

Sunday morning about seventy of the family attended a special service at the family church in Madoc, my hometown. As the beautiful music of the chimes sounded from this stately gray stone church set high on a hill overlooking the town, people arrived for worship. It became a time of celebration in many ways, an ecumenical experience in a Presbyterian church. The United Church minister acted as host and brought his congregation with him; Dudley, a Methodist, preached; one of our nephews read the scripture lesson; young men from the family ushered, and a niece sang a solo.

In the afternoon over eighty persons picnicked at a family cottage on the town's lake, where we enjoyed swimming, boating, water skiing, eating, and a big campfire on the shore at night. Watching the reflection of the campfire in the water, we talked of the many events of our lives—stories of hunting, fishing, humorous and tragic episodes that brought laughter and even tears as a reminder of our close ties with one another. We knew the greatness of the family which had no isolation; the celebration included all those who had become a part of it through the years, whether living or dead. This celebration showed our total life in community as we experienced it in the dance, eating, worship, sports, and sharing the stories and traditions with young and older generations.

I had not taken any drugs for cancer for a year, but I went every few weeks for a checkup. On one of my regular visits in mid-September, the doctor had discovered a small node on the right side of my neck. I did not ask him any questions, and he did not say anything at that time since he knew about our anniversary plans and Dudley's proposed trip around the world. Only after the celebration and when Dudley had left did we face the situation and decide on the best course of action. I again began the previous routine of blood tests each week and the injection of the cancer drug. I valued time given to me to resolve in my own mind this apparent regression. When I mentioned it to John casually, he tossed it off as nothing; both our daughters did the same, reinforcing my conviction that this should not become a crisis.

The awareness grew within me that the disease was no longer a part of my true self. I began to think of it as something literally passing away from me. I knew that the former near-death experience was something I would not be required to go through again.

If this new growth spread so that I could no longer inhabit this body and effectively live here on earth, I knew that my spirit body would emerge to its larger life. I accepted and welcomed that possibility. If, on the other hand, the growth remained small and diminished, then I would emerge to a new phase of my life here in this earth consciousness. I also accepted and welcomed that possibility.

I questioned neither the goodness nor the healing power of God. My willingness to understand and accept in new depth was challenged; so were my insights into what I had to relinquish to receive healing. This healing involved a much deeper nature than the physical and became a process which would go on as long as I inhabited this body. In this way I became part of all humanity as I sought to open myself to the light. It had never been a question of whether or not God would heal me, but rather a case of my being able to receive on all levels so a balance could be established and maintained. If we had known the truth, my system may have always lacked certain vitamins and minerals that would have assisted in establishing the necessary physical balance. Believing this, I have continued to search to find the proper foods for my diet. As I accepted the discipline of the mind and spirit through concentration and meditation, so I have diligently sought revelation on the care of my physical body, both in food intake and healthy exercise.

While Dudley traveled, I started weekly dancing lessons. When he returned we continued our lessons together, finding them a wonderful form of mental and physical relaxation. In addition, I took a concrete step toward mastering a system I had for many years followed in private; I started my first yoga instruction under an excellent teacher from India. These lessons were invaluable, but also brought some new experiences such as going into a ladies' dressing room and exposing my body while putting on leotards, realizing the age gap between myself and the average young woman taking the course, staying with it and learning that it is not a matter of body perfection or age but a real desire to bring the body into healthy exercise without strain or competition that counts. Through daily practice my body responded and I found that I could attain most of the positions. Not only did this serve a purpose physically, but also I could find a greater sense of total harmony, especially as I coordinated the movement of body with the great affirmations of the mind and spirit. Learning through relaxation and controlled breathing the art of concentration and meditation is a reward of unlimited blessings. In losing myself I found a larger self, not through isolation or withdrawal, but through the flow and movement of the whole being by coming into harmonious relationship with others and with the universe. I was the only member of the original group who completed the entire year's course.

The true adventure in so many of these experiences has been the fact that the initial stages of guidance would come to me quietly by the Spirit. But in time I verified that guidance by information received on earth. I could cite many examples of this in all aspects of my life. In the correct method of relaxation, the control of breath, the ease of contemplation achieved from the lotus (yoga) position of the body, all of which I learned in the spirit before I had the opportunity either to see or study them.

The same thing occurred in the guidance of diet. I learned to obey the voice within me. When, for example, I prepared to make the coffee I enjoyed so much one morning, the Spirit told me to drink no more of it. I obeyed. In my obedience at that moment all my former desire for coffee left me. In giving it up, I felt no tension, no difficulty in serving it to others, no reaction that would detract from their enjoyment. I obeyed something for which, at the time, I had no explanation. Later a doctor told me that he would recommend that I did not drink coffee.

One morning I awakened and a single word, at first indistinct, seemed to fill the atmosphere. I listened and tried to tune my conscious mind to the message. Slowly it came and took the form of the word "ascorbic." As I lay there it seemed such a strange word, and I did not associate it with vitamins or comprehend the implication. In my periods of meditation and in asking for illumination regarding this word, I realized that this was vitamin C. The message told me to greatly increase my present dosage.

The Healing Ministry at Foundry Church was now in its third year with living, vital experiences for an increasing number of people in study, prayer, intercession, meditation, silence, therapy, and healing worship. One of the tasks is to set up ahead of time the schedule for the meditation series, three a year, in fall, winter, and spring. I sought guidance on the new series of meditations. These themes have, in essence, always been received in the spirit. As I waited in the silence for this guidance, it became closely intertwined with my personal search for help. When a sheaf of wheat appeared before my eyes, I did not in any way see the relevance. As it daily kept appearing before my eyes, I finally took it into consciousness and accepted it.

Later I saw the sheaf of wheat with these words above it, "Taste—See—God is Good," written in large bold writing, seeming to indicate command and strength. Always they came in radiance and the wheat appeared full, bursting with life. At first I thought those words would never be accepted as the heading of the new series. What, after all, did a grain of wheat have to do with the healing ministry? But the day came also when it became a part of me, and with it came full acceptance.

At work in the kitchen one afternoon, preparing dinner, I began to see pictures before my eyes. I grabbed a piece of paper and a pencil and started to put them down in picture form. I saw fourteen scenes from the Bible, both Old and New Testaments; all that remained for me to do was look up the scripture references. The pictures equaled the exact number of Sundays and each referred to wheat in some way. This became our winter-to-Easter series.

Once I had accepted this guidance and released it for others to use, my own personal search began. I had given the meditations when either one of the ministers was out of town. I felt led to relinquish this along with several other responsibilities, and begin in earnest the search regarding the message contained for me in the grain of wheat. I read all I could find on wheat, daily opening my mind on all levels to the Spirit. One of my weekly visits to the hospital lab reminded me of the importance of the time element. The young nurse at the desk looked up and said, "Oh no, not you again." This shook me from the acceptance of a procedure that could become enslaving. For the first time in months, I began to question the blood tests and injections, and I knew a change must come soon if I were to live. The blood count began to drop dangerously, and the doctors decided to stop the chemotherapy injections.

One afternoon a friend invited me to attend a lecture on foods which dealt with specific areas of health. Later, I spoke with the lecturing doctor, who during our conversation said, "What you need are wheat sprouts." I replied, "I know, but how do I get them?" Later in the week the doctor sent me the name of a woman who grows wheat sprouts, and Dudley and I soon visited the house in Georgetown.

Never shall I forget the sight as we walked into this room, the sun streaming in the windows, lighting a table full of luscious green wheat sprouts alive with life and vitality. We watched as the woman placed the seeds on a tray to sprout, planted the sprouted ones, and showed us the method of caring for them until ready for use. How joyful I felt when the lady lifted up a tray and handed it to me. I heard the voice within say, "Taste—see—God is good." The outward expression of thanks was multiplied a hundredfold by the witness within and around me. We returned home with a bag of seed, beautiful earth in which to plant them, and a confirmation of new life and hope.

Unable to find any trays, we used what equipment we had, even oven liners, to begin our project. I spent that evening organizing what in the months ahead became a daily procedure—sifting the soil, planting the wheat, waiting, and watching the growth. I found it best to put the wheat sprouts through a meat grinder and then squeeze the juice out through a sieve. I combined this with the vegetable, parsley, watercress drink that I had used for years. My system accepted the new infusion of life with an increase of energy and strength. Not only could I handle the extra work involved in the home project, but I also had time to assist in the work of the project in Georgetown, and in this way I shared it with others.

The wheat sprouts grew well in my home during the winter and spring months, but the hot humidity of summertime in Washington did not aid their growth. At this time I learned about grass pills, which are a balanced combination of wheat, oats, barley, and rye sprouts. These pills are known by the name of Vi-et and consist of dehydrated cereal grasses which are grown outside in large fields and then processed in laboratories in Kansas City, Missouri, into tablets and powdered form. They have been used many years by Dr. E. Stanley Jones, and he tells about them in his autobiography. I found that they supplemented the wheat juice, and I made the transition to them both out of necessity and also to obtain a better balance of sprouts. At no time did I think of this as a cure for cancer, but purely as a means of needed nutrition in a form which my system could accept.

Although in the fall of 1968 I again had to begin chemotherapy, I could now take that calmly. Even when the doctor recommended the drug which I had previously rejected, I accepted his direction. I had resolved the thought of loss of my hair and was no longer fearful. The knowledge I had gained in nutrition helped, and my belief was reinforced. I experienced no loss of hair.

At this time, one of the most drastic changes in my life took place as I sought the Lord for guidance through weeks of the intense pain which had started again. The message came with authority so I could not deny or disobey. I was to cease all outside activity in the Prayer and Health work, but to continue in my daily prayer time for the sick, go once a week to Communion at the Cathedral, and otherwise release all churchgoing and work. This seemed like changing the course of a river flowing in one direction over many years. Once I had followed this direction, I asked the Lord what he wanted me to do.

"Take a brush and paint."

I remembered that I had enjoyed art in high school but had done nothing about it all these years. I began to search for a course I could take and inquired at colleges and universities. Finally one hot summer day, I stood in line with all types of young people for two hours to register for a basic drawing course at the Corcoran School of Art in downtown Washington. I had taken the last of my personal savings out of the bank to pay for my tuition the first semester. The course was for four hours, two mornings a week.

Thus a new dimension of my life began to unfold. I found enjoyment, release, excitement in this flow of creative energy under a fine instructor. I gained a new appreciation for many of the class members who at first appeared very arty and "far out." Several of them had studied in other countries; others were completing their college degrees in art in preparation to teach. Many of the more creative ones seemed at a loss to know the direction which their talent should take. I found great joy in the field trips, and the homework assignments kept me busy between classes. I also began to read and study books about great works of art and gained an appreciation of the lives and struggles of men who had once been only a name to me.

In these months I separated myself from phone calls and from former contacts. I had to center all my energy in my family, home, and the art work. As in former times of change, this was no denial of life, people, or interests, but rather it was another time when a new creative energy and expression began to flow from the center of my inner life. Time and training would be required for its direction.

At this writing the first semester work is now complete; I have attended all the classes and made good grades on my assignments. I look forward to the next step, the study of painting. Gradually I have seen the rightness of the guidance which led me in this direction. I have found the beauty of all creation, a new awareness of beauty and form, an honesty of comprehending that which I was requested to draw. This was really a confrontation with my perfectionism, for I had to achieve a gradual release from the tightness in the lines of my drawing. To be able to put something on paper as I really saw it required a greater degree of truth and comprehension than I had been willing to express. I discovered my years of contemplation and meditation were all a part of my preparation for this moment in my life.

Through all these years when things seemed to turn back on me, one thing has never changed in principle, only grown clearer and more sure. That is God's love for me. It seems beyond all comprehension—the amazing way he reaches through with a new direction and helps! The one condition is, as always, absolute trust and obedience even though I can see only one step ahead. A door will open, light will come in, and life will move forward in new power. I know that in his sight I have great value because I am his child; always and ever he wills for me total healing. I believe I am learning more about what it means to yield, to receive, not only for others but for myself. I and the Father are one.

11 | SOME CLOSING
REFLECTIONS

For Dudley and me this story has its own intrinsic meaning. It may provide some insights for others. Since we have been so thoroughly involved with each other over these twenty-five years, our reflections may be different from those others make. Whatever happens, however, we hope that some direction will come to those who have read as they pursue their own search for meaning.

We both recognize how limited and often perverse we have been for our own good and that of others. We could have avoided many of the struggles, emotional and physical, if we had known at an earlier time the wisdom available to all who seek. We are grateful for the days of growth and change which God has given to us. We accept each one as a precious trust which we must value supremely, live with zest, and devote to joy and service.

For Dudley and me one of the supreme realities is that a way of knowing and of comprehension exists which is not entirely dependent upon rational processes or mental skill. Spiritual intuition comes from an increasingly close relationship to the center of one's life and the power beyond man's physical and mental capacity. For us, the only God, the only Christ, we have truly is the one within. While the biblical record, theological discussions, and philosophical inquiry make distinctive contributions to spiritual understanding, the reality of God in Christ is known supremely in one's interior life.

Our intellectual and emotional questions about God were answered when we began to realize and affirm that prayer is something more than liturgical form, an expected custom, or a comforting formality.

We found that, despite emotional and spiritual limitations, it is possible to open the subconscious and unconscious minds to the light of spiritual forces and to find release from and utilization of the fantastic storehouse of events, experiences, people, and memories buried beyond the depths of our own mental capacities. This experience, in which we have felt a melting down of many limitations, along with a transcendence over them, has helped us face life more honestly and recognize that our human pretensions are shallow and self-defeating.

The assurance that the physical, emotional, spiritual, and social must all be integrated into the total fabric of life did not come easily. But operating on this assumption, we have realized first hand that all life is sacred, that even the sordid can be transmuted into beauty. The therapeutic value of suffering was experienced only in relation to all of life; it cannot be isolated from moments of triumph and elation. The search for spiritual reality, which began almost against our wills and wishes, became a great adventure nourishing vocational goals and the investment of full personal capacities.

Humor becomes a necessary ingredient for a decent perspective, particularly in regard to one's own pretensions and idiosyncrasies. If a person does apply this to herself or himself, it helps in viewing the patterns of institutional life in which my husband and I have been so deeply involved, particularly in reference to the church. We love it and give all to serve it, our mother in the faith. But quirks, sanctions, and rigidities which could wreck any purely human organism have plagued the church. The moralism which has characterized its life, and especially our own United Methodist Church, is obviously incompatible with the essential nature of God's universe of freedom, joy, openness, and even tragedy. Hope and love, mixed heavily with suffering and humor, are essential for growth, for us and for it.

The affirmation that life is a principle and a continuity, not an isolated event or even a series of events, is now our witness. This means that win or lose, live or die, in health or illness, with wealth or poverty, the entire drama holds eternal meaning which may have begun for us personally in the timeless age before we arrived on this planet, and will go on for eons of time ahead of us.

We know with conviction and affirm with joy:

> *God is light in our lives;*
> *God is power in our lives;*
> *God is health in our lives;*
> *God is love in our lives.*
> *God is our life!*

epilogue
THIS HOUSE
IS FULL OF JOY

For several years Alice had said that her fifty-fifth year would be a turning point, probably the most significant in her life. During the summer of 1968 we realized that we were moving to another crisis with cancer. Toward the end of August we knew that Alice would either experience a complete freedom here from the physical devastation of the disease or would be released into a new consciousness.

With these realizations, we made certain decisions—negatively, no hospitalization, no surgery, no cobalt. Positively, we would follow appropriate discipline and care of the body, both in medication and diet, and would care for each other, understanding that our main responsibility was complete unity in this care without the intrusion of any outside person or influence. Alice made it clear that she would not die from the disease lying down, that she would remain in full command of her life, that when the time came she would voluntarily release her spirit.

The confirmation that this was the best course for us came later, one Sunday evening during the healing service at Foundry Church. As I knelt at the high altar, finishing verbal intercessions, the congregation entered a period of profound silence. Then, clearly and sharply defined, I heard a most beautiful voice: "Dudley, you are greatly honored and privileged to have the opportunity to care for and minister to one so close to God."

This became the central theme of my life until March 15, 1969, when Alice took her journey.

As she had done always, Alice knew that in facing a new situation she would have to make strategic decisions and begin to move in at least one new direction. Certain things became apparent to her. For example, she felt we had to complete this book, and she also had to write the essential content of a new book, relating her many experiences as a sensitive, one whose deep spiritual perception and psychological insights had helped many people whose story she has told in a simple, beautiful style. It was also important to understand the growth and general direction of the lives of our three children.

One of Alice's most typical decisions was to enroll in the Corcoran School of Art in September, 1968, for courses in creative art, which she continued until the end, completing the last work two days before her passing. In these courses she found a new movement of life and spirit in a radically different atmosphere, and here no one was concerned about her health. Even more profoundly, she believed that a skill she had always had should come to some expression so that in her new freedom here, or in her new consciousness, a different dimension of her life might have genuine expression.

On two days during this period we knew that her life was moving toward the new consciousness. One was Christmas night. Christmas with the family had been a wonderful time. Alice had spent many weeks preparing her own special decorations for the home, including the largest and most beautiful tree we had ever had. On Christmas Eve when Beverly, our daughter arrived home from New York and walked into the hallway, she literally screamed with joy, "I have never seen anything as beautiful in all my life."

Christmas night, however, Alice and I knew that a change had taken place in her physical body, and we spent the night caring for a new development. We also knew on Valentine's Day; after lovely preparations for a family party, we realized that, for the first time, the edema had become critical.

With these changes we entered into a period when Alice suffered sustained hours of intense pain, times in which she offered her suffering as a gift of grace. We often ended these trying periods, as we did one beautiful morning, by looking at each other, laughing heartily, and saying, "How could two people go through such a messy situation and have so much fun?"

One of the most blessed moments of these months occurred one morning at 4:00 A.M. After a long night of suffering, constant care, and mutual communion, Alice, feeling some relief, sat in her own special style of regal beauty and gave one of the most beautiful meditations on the relationship of suffering and grace that I have ever heard.

Our Holy Week began on March 8 and concluded on March 15. On March 8, as I left for my class and the service in the healing ministry at Foundry, Alice called me.

"Dudley, I have written two letters to you. One is for the memorial service at Foundry, and the other for the funeral service at home in Madoc. The whole point of these letters is to liberate you, as you deal with this matter, with the large family who will need to understand my wishes."

The main themes expressed in these letters were joy, hope, lively music, color, beautiful flowers, and the triumphant recognition that life is continuity and grows in the new consciousness. Her concluding paragraph, which discussed the funeral service in Madoc, was characteristic: "Have a meal together, and fun, because I will be there in spirit, very gay and bright."

157

For the next five nights a most unusual thing happened. On each of those nights we had five hours of uninterrupted sleep, something which had not occurred for months; but during this week we felt the great sense of peace, hope, and joy.

A month before, as I sat alone in our living room, I noticed our twenty-fifth anniversary picture which had just been taken. I wondered if the photographer could extract Alice's picture from the portrait, making one of only her. I called the photographer, and he said it would be difficult to block me out of the photograph, but he would try.

On Tuesday of our Holy Week the picture was delivered to my office, and I took it home in the large carton.

"Alice, I have a surprise for you. Would you like it before or after dinner?"

"I think I need a lift now. Let me have it before dinner."

When I showed her the carton, she could not imagine what it was; but as we began to open it, she said, "It's a picture," still not realizing what it was. When she saw it, she was completely overwhelmed and deeply touched.

"Dudley, nothing that you could have done would have made life better than this."

Later that evening, as she rested, I went upstairs and found her looking at this beautiful picture. "Is it a sin to look at something which is yourself and call it beautiful?" she asked. I replied, "Of course not."

Then she said: "Really, the most important thing about this is that I now feel at peace and have no longer any concern about your potential spiritual growth. You received a spiritual insight and without hesitation acted on it, and the result is this beautiful experience which expresses love, beauty, and spiritual vitality, and I am happy."

Friday morning, March 14, Alice, remembering that no one came to our home during the day, spoke to me as I left for my office.

"Dudley, I want you to know that if anything should happen to me, or if I should faint when you are not here, do not feel badly. No other could have cared and given the time and effort that you have over these months."

When I came home at noon, as I had done for some time each day except when traveling, to shower her and prepare her lunch, things seemed a little different. I did not want to go back to the office. However, just before leaving the office I had received a phone call from someone who said, "I'm ready to commit suicide." I had told that person to come at once to my office and if at all possible, I would get back. Two other persons came to see me that day, and I realized that even in the midst of our own new circumstances, service to others must go on. This was what Alice wished.

Returning home that afternoon at five, I knew Alice's condition had worsened. I could not get our regular doctor to check her and to see that I was doing everything wise and necessary. I was able to contact Dr. Harvey Ammerman, an outstanding neurosurgeon and close personal friend, who came by and confirmed that her toxic condition had intensified. He returned later that evening, and I did report to the doctor standing in for our regular doctor.

That night, as I had done many nights before, I brought the foam rubber mattress from my study couch, laid it on the floor, and rested there. Every few minutes Alice and I worked together, attempting to make things as comfortable as possible. Despite the discomfort, it was a beautiful night. For during those hours of sleeplessness, the realization grew within us that this was to be a crucial and exhilarating day. In some peculiar way we were preparing for an advent.

At 5:30 in the morning I arose, greeted by a beautiful, fresh spring day with the birds singing and the fragrance from the flowering trees penetrating the entire room. I bathed, shaved, and dressed, and then proceeded to clear the entire room of all the evidence, which was very little, of medicine and other items connected with illness, carefully assembled the drafting and art material, put the mattress away so that the room was clean, orderly, and lively with the vibrations of the new life bursting all around. From 5:30 until 7:00 we visited about many things.

At 7:00 Alice said to me, "Dudley, I would like to walk over and sit in the rocker which I have used over these months for my art and writing." So we took the long walk to the rocker. I realized, after she had been sitting there awhile, that she was suffering, and I told her we must return to the bed. It was an even longer trip back. Once she almost stumbled, and I prayed firmly within myself that nothing would happen which would undercut any of her personal dignity and command. At 7:00 I called the stand-in doctor, asking him to stop at the house on his way to the hospital just to check that we were doing all that we should under the circumstances.

At 7:30 he came by. I had not seen him before, and neither had Alice. As I introduced him to her, she said brightly and clearly, "Doctor, it's a great thing to be alive."

The person whom he had come to attend, a person he thought was dying, responded as though he were treating someone with a simple cold. It was a refreshing thing to watch his change of attitude and response.

He did say that he thought we needed help that day, perhaps a nurse, and at least some hypos. As I took him to the door, Alice called me. She didn't want anyone, especially a stranger, to consult about her condition outside of her presence.

From 8:00 until about 8:15 we had a beautiful talk, and Alice said, "We don't need the kind of help the doctor is speaking about. No one could have done more than you have done. Let us be together and love each other for as long as we can. Furthermore, my help is coming quickly and it is very beautiful."

At 8:15 she asked me for a glass of juice. I went to get it and she kidded me for bringing a long glass with a short straw. At precisely 8:28 she spoke softly.

"Dudley, it is now time for me to get up and for us to sit together and talk."

I helped her from the bed, and we sat with our feet firmly on the floor.

"Which side would you like me to sit on?"

"You always sit on my left side, which is close to my heart, when we are to talk and pray," she replied. I noticed the contract for this book on my dresser, and said, "We will complete that today."

At 8:30, as we began a prayer, Alice's head dropped on my shoulder. She was gone.

We sat there for five minutes together, her body still warm. Then I laid her back in bed, covered her to her neck, and moved to the chair in which she had sat an hour before. There for a half hour I had the greatest experience of my life, for I knew that all was light and beauty and that the spirits and the angels had come. If I had never believed in the ministry of angels before, I certainly did then, and now. The house was *full of joy*, of vitality. The spirits of her father and mother and my father, and a host of others, were there to take her and walk with her, and to minister to me.

Later, I called the doctors to tell them. Dr. Ammerman left his breakfast, came and confirmed the reality. Then Dr. Nicholas, who had been there two hours before, arrived, and as they both entered the bedroom, they said simultaneously, "This house is alive, it is a beautiful time." We talked for awhile and looked at her portrait.

"You know, this has been such a wonderful experience," Dr. Nicholas said. "I had never seen this woman before, but I realize that this is different, and I hope that if anything like this should happen in our home, it would be like this."

It had happened in a most unusual way, and as we wanted it,

in our own home, our own bedroom, sitting up, no other person in the home (as the children were on vacation), with dignity and command, for Alice had released her spirit voluntarily as she had said she would, and with great assurance moved into her new consciousness and all the wonders of her new existence.

One great quality of her life was an element of beautiful mystery, which I shall always miss and yet remember with joy. It was evidenced again immediately after she had gone. As I stripped the bed after they had taken her body, I observed, as I had many times before during the last few months, that in a simple plain cotton cloth she had the silver horseshoe which her father had made as a blacksmith in his youth. With this silver horseshoe she had put some dry crusts of bread.

Alice would have had a longer, detailed, deeply spiritual reason for this. However, I knew what it all meant. The horseshoe represented identification with her family, strong persons who worked hard, and also with the great created world of animals and all living things. The dry crusts represented God's provision for life, for its sustenance and for its hope. This quality of mystery which was always associated with Alice remains for me one of the most intriguing aspects of her total existence and so much a part of our joint search for spiritual vitality.

So it continued. The realization of the human loss and the agony which it brings, and the exhilaration of a great new spiritual joy.

The children wished to see her remains just before they were shipped to Canada. Alice had given strict instruction that there should be no public viewing. However, on the Sunday afternoon and on the Tuesday evening before the service the children and I visited the funeral director's parlor and there, alone, viewed these mortal remains, described so beautifully by Dianne in a letter which came on Easter Saturday evening:

162

How does one contain the tremendous sense of excitement generated while gazing at a body in perfect peace and knowing so very surely that it remains only as the delicate shell of a living, vibrant soul?

We experienced all of the strange combination of sadness and grief, and joy and hope. We cried, deeply, fully, expressively, but our tears were interlaced with great laughter and joy as we contemplated the reality and the earthiness—and the essential humanness of this person whom we loved so much.

We remembered her penetrating sharpness when it was appropriate, her laughter, and her zest for joy, for pleasure, and the sensitive care and ingenuity with which she managed her home, especially as it showed in her capacity to entertain with a flare. So lively was our laughter as we recalled so many exciting things that the funeral director and other persons in the home came by to look at such a strange group. But this is the way it was, and the way it had always been.

We knew the joy in the tea on Tuesday afternoon before the memorial service in Washington, when about 125 friends and neighbors came to enjoy the beauty, wonder, and vitality of the occasion. It was evidenced also as the families gathered for the memorial service which was one of joy and hope, in which distinguished leaders of the church participated. It was true in the funeral service in Madoc, so charged with feelings of both grief and joy.

We knew as a family, and all knew, that we were entering into a new phase of life with the benediction of her wonderful life behind us and continually with us.

"Isn't it wonderful that the life of the Spirit is so close and she is at the heart of it," Beverly has written. John has smiled and said, "This was exactly the way it would be," when I told him of her spiritual visit to the home on the first morning that I was alone again.

163

Our note of acknowledgment sent to friends and relatives included a verse which Alice had copied in her own strong handwriting, for her own use, on the Thursday evening before she journeyed. From "Joy Is Like the Rain," sung by the Medical Mission Sisters of Philadelphia, the verse expresses so well Alice's life and its unique and living qualities.

> I saw raindrops on my window,
> Joy is like the Rain,
> Laughter runs across my pain,
> Joy is like the Rain. . . .
> I saw Christ in wind and thunder,
> Joy is tried by Storm.
> Christ asleep within my boat,
> Whipped by wind yet still afloat.
> Joy is tried by Storm.[1]

I know with assurance and declare with conviction that "this house is full of joy."

---

[1] © 1965 by Medical Mission Sisters. Publisher: Vanguard Music, N.Y., N.Y.; from Album No. AVS101. Avant Garde Records Inc., 250 W. 57th St., N.Y., N.Y.; Chappell & Co. Ltd., Toronto.

appendix
THE MINISTRY OF
PRAYER AND HEALTH

The Ministry of Prayer and Health at Foundry United Methodist Church in the nation's capital stands as a memorial to the life of Alice Ward.

Within the massive stone walls of this old inner-city church in Washington, D.C., a small group of disciplined people has for a number of years practiced a modern approach to prayer and health which could possibly affect the state of the entire world. Based on fundamental Christian principles of worship and backed by centuries of Christian tradition in the healing ministry, the philosophy of this "redeemed fellowship of believers" is, nevertheless, unique for this century and dedicated to the renewal of a functional interrelationship among all healing processes, including the spiritual.

In our present culture the reaction to the term "spiritual healing" is often hotly negative, notes Dr. Edward W. Bauman, senior minister of Foundry Church. "Many people are frightened or angered by the 'fanatical' approach to healing, and as a church we are opposed to it also, which is not say that we discount any results of this

---

This is an adaptation of the article "Ministry of Prayer and Health" by Mary Pat Pugh, which appeared in *Church and Home*, September, 1968. Copyright © 1968 by the Board of Publication of The Evangelical United Brethren Church.

more exaggerated form of 'faith healing.' We simply believe there is a better way."

That "better way" has been manifested in the efforts of about forty disciplined members of Foundry Church, participants in intercessory prayer and study groups, the foundation of the healing ministry. "The ministry is dedicated to wholeness through the power of God," explains Dr. Bauman, who visualizes a renaissance of interest and participation in the endeavor to bring about comprehensive healing through prayer, meditation, and intellectual and spiritual striving toward God.

"People everywhere are rediscovering the ancient disciplines of the mind and spirit which have enabled man to attain superior levels of intellect and perception, to achieve communication with God," Dr. Bauman comments, adding that the Ministry of Prayer and Health at Foundry contains characteristics which resemble many empirical philosophies but which is totally unique in its particular combination of hypotheses. "We're still searching for explicit definity of our own philosophy of spiritual healing."

Early in his ministry at Foundry, Dr. Bauman and a few others committed to and experienced in the healing ministry discussed the possibility of a carefully planned, authentically mandated and officially approved ministry of prayer and health. A few persons gathered to express interest, met for several weeks, finally received the endorsement of the Official Board and were organized as a Committee on Prayer and Health. Co-chairmen of this group were Dr. and Mrs. A. Dudley Ward; Dr. Ward is general secretary of the Board of Christian Social Concerns of The United Methodist Church. Alice Ward was unofficially acknowledged as the guiding force of the group since it was largely through her influence that the group had been formed with so much diversity and that it had acquired such a high level of discipline.

"One of the fascinating parts of the entire venture is that the people who have been most deeply involved are those who have needed this ministry the most," Alice Ward observed before her death in 1969. "In a common search for wholeness and reality we

166

have found that in our own deep personal needs there has come both redemption and health. This is a sort of built-in validity to the soundness of the ministry as it has developed."

Five specific areas comprise the Ministry of Prayer and Health which clearly professes to "cooperate fully with medical and psychiatric techniques and praise God for all who are ministers to health." The five interrelated ingredients are:

The study of the meaning of prayer and health (involving the use of certain books and other written materials instructing in the disciplines of prayer and meditation and acquainting the students with medical, theological, and psychological insights into the behavior of man).

Intercession-meditation prayer groups (composed of those people who have completed two courses in the study and meaning of prayer), whose basic purpose is to pray for the healing of persons (their spiritual and physical wholeness) and the healing of the world (in the full dynamic sense).

The daily discipline of meditation and silence (practiced by the most "accomplished" of the intercessory prayer group).

Personal counseling and group therapy by the Washington Pastoral Counseling Service. (Each participant in therapy is required to take a written psychological examination which is clinically evaluated by a psychologist who, in turn, consults with the "patient" and often offers suggestions for therapy.)

Healing services (confession, praise and thanksgiving, prayer for healing, sacred vocal and instrumental music and the sacrament of laying-on of hands all compose the various elements of these services).

The healing services are open to the entire community and involve the full congregation in prayer and verbal participation. The ancient sacrament of the laying-on of hands is administered individually and only to those who have consulted with the ministers of prayer and health. The sacrament itself is administered in an atmosphere of profound solemnity and deeply conscientious worship following an extended period of silence; the meditative drama is climaxed by the benediction.

The sacrament is a relatively new variation in the healing service since several obstacles prevented its rapid initiation into the format: the clergy had to be adequately prepared to offer this blessing, first and foremost; then the congregation had to be taught the true purpose and proper attitude toward the sacrament so that a receptive and contributive atmosphere could be achieved for the sacrament event; certain guidelines had to preclude the sensationalism and the false expectancies so common in such services. The following are the provisions which appear on the special order of worship prepared for the laying-on of hands:

"This sacrament is a blessing made possible by God through the Holy Spirit and the offices of the church. It is an ancient rite and central to early Christian experience made plain in the New Testament by Jesus and the Apostles. The church has ministered in this way for a variety of purposes such as the ordination of clergy, the blessing of children, and in its healing work.

"For the Prayer and Health Ministry at Foundry, it signifies at least the following for the congregation and those who have expressed the desire for this blessing and have been in consultation with the clergy.

"For the one receiving the blessing, his is a dedication to practice faithfully the spiritual disciplines of prayer, meditation, study and worship; to utilize fully all those appropriate healing ministries of medicine (including preventative nutritional therapy), psychiatry and the spiritual. (A course of six lectures on modern methods of nutrition were given by the Ministry of Prayer and Health in the spring of 1968 by a medical doctor.)

"For the church it means that the clergy are the instruments by which God's healing power and love are transmitted in an act of worship and dedication. It also means that both the clergy and the congregation assume the responsibility of continued prayerful support and love."

The focal point of any Foundry healing service, however, is the celebration of prayer at the prayer desk (for the assembled congregation) and at the high altar for the "prayer list," a compilation of the first names of those who have signed a request for prayer and for whom the intercessory prayer group has been praying. The list is read by either Dr. Ward or Dr. Bauman at the high altar where special intercession is made. The opportunity is given for the congregation audibly to submit additional names to the list at this time. Many parishioners come on invitation to the altar and also engage in personal prayer while intercession is underway.

Membership and participation in one of the prayer or study groups is acquired through weeks of preparation and study, and, in the case of the intercessory prayer groups, members are subject to the scrutiny and constructive criticism of their peers during that period when they are attempting to achieve the proper communication with God and to establish a dynamic means of praying for humanity.

"We'll help anyone who is willing to make a diligent effort to become involved with Christ," Alice Ward said in 1968. Her own involvement in the Foundry Ministry of Prayer and Health was unique and highly significant. Alice Ward's desire to help instigate a health-through-prayer program at her church was a direct result of her own experiences with pain, suffering, and the prospect of death. She through physical and emotional anguish felt that man can draw near to Christ and commence to affirm and receive divine love in his life.

"Since I was a child I have felt the power of God's influence in my entire being," Alice recalled. "I have always discerned an intimate rapport with Christ, but it was not until I approached death three times that I realized how strongly this divine current could operate in my life. I wanted to cause others to realize that each man is responsible for his own state of conscience, his own life, and let them know that I offer my hand to help guide them to developing their own communication with God."

Alice had, in the course of helping organize the study and prayer groups, literally summoned certain people to the membership of these groups, saying that it was God's will and command (transmitted through her). Physicians, lawyers, scholars, executives, men in the armed forces, maids, secretaries (of all races and of many religious persuasions) have joined the groups, have grown into and with them and, without exception, testify to "tremendous personal improvements," especially "in the lives who protested that they wouldn't in their wildest dreams belong in a group having such a purpose," Alice noted.

The philosophy which forms the basis for the study groups of the Ministry of Prayer and Health seems to draw from many empirical philosophies and carries with it allusions to literary and philosophical analogies of many genres (e.g. transcendentalism, Platonism, etc.); but it remains generally concluded that the Foundry thesis is a Christian concept and seems in many instances to be reminiscent of other philosophies simply because Christianity (the teachings of Jesus, specifically) has been the model for a significant number of philosophical theories. It is, of course, no point of debate that many of the principles of Christianity are shared by several other religious philosophies.

Alice Ward articulated the prime syllabus on the premise that man is a dynamic being composed of spirit, physical body, intellect and emotion. As such, man must be studied and dealt with in reference to his illnesses, adversities, personality changes and neuroses in terms of his dynamic make-up.

In approaching man's problems by considering the whole man whose various facets of his being contribute to the state of his mind and body and spirit, human beings gain a wider insight into the behavior of man and into his basic spiritual needs and longings as well. With this foundation concept in mind a second major postulate is interposed: that through each man runs the current of God's love, the force of divine action in his life. Through study, prayer, meditation and discipline, it is possible for a man to develop to a high degree that vestige of the "God within" himself. Through intimate communication with God, man can become capable of invoking the power of God on behalf of other individuals to whose "God within" he appeals in prayer. Thus, man can work constructively to improve the state of his fellowman and, simultaneously, improve his own state of being by striving to perfect his spiritual life and, in so doing, becoming receptive to the will of God, the direction and comfort and peace afforded by God.

"A religious experience, however profound, does not at one blow solve the problems of a person's life," cautions Dr. Paul Tournier, whose books the group studies, "but such an experience does nevertheless show how closely a person's physical and psychological state depends on victories which are won only in the realm of the spirit."

Dr. Bauman reflects his concept of the solution of a man's problems in charging that "a man may not be cured completely of his disease when he dies, but he may die a healed man because his soul has become whole and healed."

The prayer list (composed of an average of seventy-five names per week) provided to the Intercessory Prayer Group is made up of names either requested by the person himself or another concerned person. Each request must be made in writing and signed. Cards are provided for this purpose. Requests must be renewed each month or the name is dropped. The last names of the prayer subjects are not given, and no discussion of disease or problem is dealt with. Often the prayer sessions begin with long periods of silent meditation.

During such times, explains Dr. Ward, the prayer group reaffirms its strength of unity and prays for the binding of the lives of those present to the spirit of God. Through such effort for communication, such trust in the grace of God, the healing power of Christ is known in the lives of those prayed for. The concept of "healing" is a tremendously comprehensive one, Dr. Bauman points out: "When we speak of healing and pray for healing, we are speaking of an amelioration of all the ills of the world, poverty, tyranny, war, greed, all the things which corrupt the ideal state of existence as held in God's vision . . . as well as for man's individual diseases and disturbances."

Often special prayers for peace and reconciliation of the races are prominent objectives of the prayer sessions in closed groups and at the altars. It is believed at Foundry that the sincere prayer of the man who loves God helps to create the atmosphere for peace.

"People come and go all the time looking for miracles," Alice Ward said. "They must learn that they need to come and learn and study and work, to see themselves honestly, to learn of the dimensions of healing."

It was obvious in conversations with Mrs. Ward that she viewed illness and adversity and death as creative forces, forces which "lay the individual bare in his emotions" and come closest to tapping that reservoir of spiritual strength which renders him receptive to the "light of God," the revelation of God in man. "If a man is willing to change," she believed, "God will enable him to do so.

171

This prayer, this affirmation is a step of faith and a move toward freedom of the spirit to concentrate on eternally valuable objectives."

Participants hope that the prayer and health ministry can become a coordinant for the various organizations in the church which wish to become engaged in intercession for people and events. It is hoped also that the number of disciplined, trained intercessors will increase to accommodate the growing number of prayer requests. A new venture will be to train persons to visit the sick and to extend the healing ministry into the hospitals and homes of persons who are in physical and emotional need. "We are also working to take greater advantage of the knowledge and capacity of medical doctors and psychiatrists who can be of very great help in relating constructively the spiritual aspects of this ministry to the physical needs of individuals," Dr. Ward further defines.

The complex nature of Foundry's Ministry of Prayer and Health, the effort and time required in the preparation for participation, preclude any rapid spread of this type of ministry throughout this and other countries. However, a few ministries of the same type are revealing themselves gradually. One such ministry is progressing now in Sarasota, Florida, under the direction of Dr. John Ennis Large, rector of St. Bonaventure Episcopal Church; Dr. Large has written a text concerning this "new wave" spiritual healing ministry, *The Church's Ministry of Healing.*

The primary question evoked by such ministry as the Prayer and Health Ministry at Foundry is, of course, "Have there been any constructive results?" The senior pastor reflects on the question and states definitely, "We can't count the number of crutches that have been thrown away, but there is no doubt in my mind that there are definite favorable results due directly to the efforts of the intercessory prayer groups. As I said before, a man may die of his illness but he may die having been made whole, having been drawn to communication with Christ, and that is victory."

Personal testimony of members of the ministry's committee and the various study and prayer groups speaks vividly of the "tremendous strength" that has come to them. "We are finding that enthusiasm, joy, inspiration and exciting adventure color all our days," said one intercessory prayer member. "Even during the summer heat we have met regularly, with no drop-outs and with new members constantly joining the ranks."

Other members testify to an increased understanding of spiritual truths, an awakening to the fact that life must have meaning and purpose. They speak of having become aware of the needs of their community and the world and of a willingness to be a channel of love and strength to others. Others speak of an increased tolerance and patience in dealing with people (thereby lessening their own tensions, irritations, and frustrations as well as those of others), of a gradually increasing selflessness. All agree that the practice of prayer and meditations have "quieted their hearts" and allowed them to realize a peace of mind and a reliance on God which they never dreamed possible.

Letters come which testify to the great healing or the power of healing which has become theirs. "The results are not numerous or necessarily dramatic, but they are sure and the direction is definitely good," observes Dr. Ward.

One object of the intercessory prayer groups' efforts was a middle-aged woman with advanced glaucoma of a twelve-year duration. She had attended the Foundry healing service a number of times and had spoken with the Wards about her spiritual longings as well as about her illness. Spiritually prepared for the imminent surgery, she entered the operating room "relaxed and with a total change in attitude." Within a day after surgery she experienced a vivid spiritual force working within her: "Both eyes bandaged, yet I could see without doubt a very strong light. It seemed to fill my entire head and it stayed all day. I was convinced that it was the healing Light of Christ which I had prayed for so many times to come into my eyes."

Within two days this woman was permitted to walk about and "everyone was amazed; the healing was progressing rapidly and I simply did not go through some things others went through." Her progress was remarkably rapid, and all traces of the glaucoma and also an accompanying detached retina complication were absent. And the patient had a fresh, ambitious lease on life, stimulated by the conversion experience of her illness.

A member of the intercessory prayer group, Mr. Neil Brooks, a Washington attorney, emphasizes the total scope of the healing that occurred in his life during convalescence after a cardiac attack.

"Last winter I experienced acute coronary insufficiency, and for many weeks I was in bed. That period was characterized not only by the frequent pains of angina pectoris, but also by deep depression, anxiety, insomnia, muscular spasms, numbness in the extremities, loss of appetite, diabetes and profound weakness. Worse than the physical illness was my spiritual impoverishment. To be sure, I had generally attended church services, but, frankly, my religious experience had been lacking in depth.

" 'A healthy body,' said Francis Bacon, 'is the guest chamber of the soul; a sick, its prison.' I certainly felt that I was in prison, and there seemed to be little, if any, basis for hope. At this juncture my wife attended the Sunday evening healing service at Foundry and requested that my name be included in the prayer list.

"My physical condition slowly improved and by mid-summer I had recovered in all respects except for the angina pectoris and mild diabetes. My need for healing, however, was for God's healing of my life in its totality. In this broad and basic consideration, I found of inestimable value (1) the classes my wife and I attended at Foundry, (2) our conversations with leaders of the healing ministry, and (3) the healing service each Sunday evening at the church.

"When I entered the hospital subsequently later, my attitude was in marked contrast to that of last winter. Although I was in the intensive care section, my wife and I were calm and confident that, in God's grace, all would be well. Our faith had been activated and strengthened by our participation in the prayer and health program at Foundry, and we had learned about effectual prayer. Instead of being anxious, we had firm faith in God's love. Drugs were not necessary to induce sleep or a tranquil state of mind. Through it all we were encouraged, greatly encouraged, by the prayers of the members of the prayer groups.

"My physical improvement in the hospital was remarkably rapid. Since leaving the hospital the progression process of recovery has continued to be accelerated." [1]

---

[1] Neil Brooks entered his new consciousness on December 26, 1969, at peace, with thanksgiving and as a whole person.

"Any success that we've had at Foundry Church is due to the faithfulness of very simple souls," Alice Ward stated before her death. Results such as those attested to at Foundry Church are subtle results, intangible triumphs exerted by the power of prayer. The prayers are being offered by a small group of people who recognized a deep void in their lives, who longed for an indefinable *something,* who studied and prayed to develop the "God within" themselves that they might relate to the "God within" their distressed and wretched fellowman. Some, through improper orientation to the task, have failed; some regress, hit plateaus of no progress, simply fail.

But others have learned a certain something which is latent in the soul of each man to know . . . if he is touched by the Holy Spirit, through his own or someone else's efforts. Some have evolved into an understanding of the power of "Light" in their lives; their perception has broadened into a knowledge of continuity, of the total span of experience, in some cases a glimmer of the comprehension of the life to come; a more acute awareness of the most minute processes of existence. Some have died confident that for the first time they are really living.

Perhaps no raucous, histrionic miracles will take place ever again; perhaps man is doomed to perish in his debauchery before he has a chance to carry out the Great Commission. But there is the comforting thought that while the pain of the entire world is screamed into the void, God is silently, in a still small voice, producing works of art in the lives of those who seek his revelation.